DEMOGRAPHY LIBRARY PSC UPENN

331967

BK
HE5613
.R37
1988

R37 1988

:hael.

the role of the
= / Michael Renner.

DEMOGRAPHY LIBRARY

JUN 2 0 1988

Introduction

Chroniclers of the auto industry credit Henry Ford with almost single-handedly reorienting the industry from custom-made vehicles for a privileged elite toward standard cars for a mass market. Assembly-line production dramatically lowered costs and brought car ownership within reach for millions of Americans. The allure of the automobile culture has since seemed unstoppable. In 1987, a record 126,000 cars rolled off assembly lines each working day, and close to 400 million vehicles clog the world's streets today.[1]

The individual mobility, comfort, and convenience that the private passenger car bestows are unparalleled by any other means of transportation. The very embodiment of modern society's infatuation with technical progress, the automobile has even been called "the greatest mobile force for freedom," and credited with promoting such lofty goals as democracy and women's liberation.[2]

The car's utility to the individual stands in sharp contrast to the costs and burdens that society must shoulder to provide an automobile-centered transportation system. Since the first automobiles rolled off assembly lines, societies have enacted a steady stream of laws to protect drivers from each other and themselves, as well as to protect the general public from the unintended effects of massive automobile use. Most such measures have initially met with resistance, and legislators have continually struggled over the competing goals of unlimited mobility and the individual's right to be free of the noise, pollution, and physical dangers that cars often bring.

Concern about the viability of the automobile system, however well-reasoned or documented, has hardly diminished its allure. Ameri-

I would like to thank Susan Norris for production assistance and John Young for spirited research support. I am grateful to Jeff Alson, Deborah Blevis, Clarence Ditlow, Ken Hughes, Philip Patterson, Michael Replogle, and Michael Walsh for reviewing early drafts of this manuscript.

cans' longstanding love affair with the automobile has proved to be contagious. Even in the Soviet Union and China, most people who can afford a car are eager to own one. In much of the Third World, the resources of entire nations are marshaled to build and maintain a transportation system that serves only a disparately small share of the population.

Prior to the seventies, the auto's utility and sustainability were hardly questioned. But a decade of gasoline lines and oil price increases left the automobile with all the momentum of Los Angeles traffic at rush hour. Then worries about escalating gas prices and future fuel availability seemed to subside in the eighties almost as quickly as they had emerged. Improved energy efficiency and additional oil supplies combined to bring fuel prices down. As a result, car sales have recovered, driving is up, and affluent customers are once more shopping for high-performance cars.

The motor vehicle industry's apparent success in dealing with the challenges of the seventies has obscured the adverse long-term trends that automobile-centered transportation is creating. Rising gasoline consumption will before long put increased pressure on oil production capacities. In the long run, supply reliance is bound to shift toward the Middle East, where by far the largest and cheapest petroleum reserves are to be found. In addition, as more and more people can afford their own cars and as mass motorization takes hold, congestion becomes an intractable problem. And motor vehicles are an important source of the air pollution that plagues cities around the world and takes an uncounted toll on human health. Pollutants from cars also contribute to the formation of acid rain and to global warming.

Society's interest in oil supply security, the integrity of its cities, and protection of the environment calls for a fundamental rethinking of the role automobiles should play. Stricter fuel economy and pollution standards are the most obvious and immediate measures that can be adopted. But they can only be part of the answer. In the years ahead, the challenge will be innovative thinking on transportation policies.

"Rising
gasoline consumption
will before long
put increased pressure on
oil production capacities."

Whither the Automotive Age?

The automotive pioneers did not foresee today's mass market, view-   7
ing the car as a leisure object for the well-to-do. In 1901, for example,
Mercedes Benz estimated the ultimate world market potential to be no
higher than 1 million cars.[3] By 1915, the industry had already crossed
that threshold, and during the twenties the car culture took root in the
United States. The depression of the thirties and the ravages of World
War II temporarily retarded further growth of car production and
ownership.

Then, during the postwar period, the automobile industry experi-
enced its most dramatic and sustained expansion, buttressed by massive highway construction projects, fueled by cheap and abundant
oil, and riding a wave of unprecedented affluence in industrial countries. Production grew at a rapid 6 percent annually, from under 10
million vehicles a year in the fifties to almost 30 million in 1973. A car
in every garage seemed not too audacious a dream.[4]

Since the abrupt onset of the first oil crisis, however, the production of
autos has entered an era of unsettling volatility. Output tumbled by
about 5 million vehicles, or almost one-fifth, during the 1974-75 reces-
sion, and by slightly less in the 1980-82 slump. (See Figure 1.) Emerg-
ing from violent ups and downs occasioned by the oil shocks of 1973
and 1979, global production reached a new peak of 32.9 million
vehicles in 1987. Yet had the pace recorded between 1950 and 1973
continued, annual output would now be twice as high.[5]

The world's car fleet has grown from about 50 million vehicles in the
immediate postwar period to 386 million in 1986. (See Table 1.) There
is still no sign of a real leveling-off in the size of the world's car fleet.
But since 1977, a growing portion of new cars in the major automobile-owning societies have been bought to replace older cars; that
share is currently well above two-thirds. If the pre-1973 pace of
additions to the car fleet—not just replacements—had held, total
passenger cars would now number close to 600 million.

Million
Vehicles

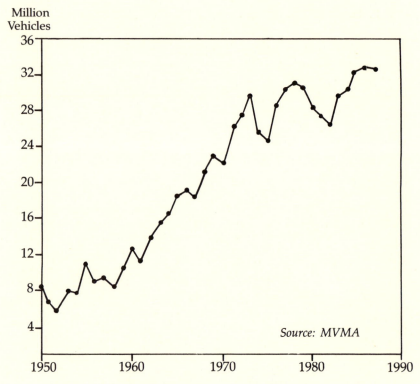

Figure 1: World Passenger Car Production, 1950–87

The United States dominated the early stages of the automotive age. Not until the late sixties did the rest of the world cumulatively own and produce more cars than the United States did. Annual U.S. production peaked in 1973, with imports claiming a steadily growing share of the American market. The country now accounts for one-quarter of the world's auto output and one-third of its car fleet.[6]

Table 1: Automobiles in Use, Worldwide and United States, 1950–86

Year	World	United States	U.S. Share
	(million passenger cars)		(percent)
1950	53	40	75
1955	73	52	71
1960	98	62	63
1965	140	75	54
1970	195	89	46
1971	207	93	45
1972	220	97	44
1973	236	102	43
1974	249	105	42
1975	260	107	41
1976	270	110	41
1977	286	114	40
1978	297	117	39
1979	310	120	39
1980	321	122	38
1981	331	123	37
1982	340	124	36
1983	352	127	36
1984	365	128	35
1985	375	132	35
1986	386	135	35

Source: Motor Vehicle Manufacturers Association, *World Motor Vehicle Data, 1988 Edition* and *Facts and Figures '88* (Detroit, Mich.: 1988).

During the fifties and sixties, Europe arose as the earliest challenger to American dominance. By 1969, combined European production surpassed that of the United States and Canada, and Western Europe also began to match the North American market in size. Japan emerged as the most dynamic producer in the seventies. From a mere 165,000 vehicles in 1960, Japan rapidly expanded its output to nearly 8 million today, rivaling the United States as the world's preeminent producer. Undoubtedly, the two oil price shocks of the seventies greatly increased the appeal of fuel-efficient Japanese cars. But high-quality manufacturing and design continue to be crucial components in the country's successful export drive. Japan also became the second largest single market after the United States: From fewer than a half million in 1960, car ownership leapt to about 28 million in 1985.[7]

Car ownership in industrial countries continues to spread, but the pace has slowed. Most people who desire a car already own one. From an annual average of 4 percent between 1950 and 1973, growth of car ownership in the United States declined to 2 percent between 1974 and 1985. A slowdown is unmistakable as well in Japan and Western Europe.[8]

Consumers in Western Europe and Japan increasingly prefer to trade in their older vehicles for larger and more luxurious models, particularly as fuel prices have declined in the eighties. In the United States, light trucks—pickups and minivans—enjoy rising popularity because they offer four-wheel drive and more loading space. In 1987, they accounted for one-third of all passenger vehicle sales. And in all industrial countries, people already owning one vehicle are eyeing a second or even a third one.[9]

Automobile production and ownership are still overwhelmingly concentrated in advanced industrial societies. (See Tables 2 and 3.) North America, Western Europe, Japan, and Oceania account for only 16 percent of the world's population but 88 percent of the car production and 81 percent of the global fleet. Put differently, by 1985 only a little more than 1 percent of the Third World's population owned a car, compared with 40 percent in the western industrial countries, and a world average of about 8 percent. Yet the lure of owning a private

"By 1985,
a little more than 1 percent
of the Third World's population
owned a car, compared with
40 percent in industrial countries."

Table 2: World Passenger Car Production, by Region, 1971–86

Region or Country	1971[1]	1980	1986
	(million vehicles)		
Western Europe	10.9	10.4	11.8
United States	8.6	6.4	7.8
Japan	3.7	7.0	7.8
Soviet Union	0.5	1.3	1.3
Latin America	0.7	1.1	1.1
Canada	1.1	0.8	1.1
Eastern Europe	0.5	1.1	1.0
Asia[2]	0.05	0.1	0.6
Oceania	0.4	0.3	0.3
World	26.5	28.5	32.8

[1]Chosen for comparative purposes because 1970 was an abnormally low year for car production in North America.
[2]Excluding Japan.

Source: Worldwatch Institute, based on Motor Vehicle Manufacturers Association, *Facts and Figures* (Detroit, Mich.: various editions).

passenger car—and the status, mobility, and better life that its possession appears to promise—seems irresistible everywhere on the globe. As soon as income allows, many people accord high priority to buying a car.[10]

Until the seventies, the Soviet Union and Eastern Europe deliberately avoided devoting their industrial potential to auto production. Traditionally, they relied on trains and buses for transportation, and gave the manufacturing of trucks priority over that of passenger cars. But in response to growing consumer pressure, passenger car production more than tripled in the seventies. Between 1970 and 1985, the Soviet and East European car fleets grew fivefold—to 27 million vehicles. The pace slowed somewhat during the first half of the eighties, but average annual growth, at 7 percent, was nevertheless more than

Table 3: Car Density in 1970–85 and Car Fleet in 1985, by Region

Region or Country	Density			1985 Fleet
	1970	1980	1985	
	(people per car)			(million vehicles)
United States	2.0	1.9	1.8	132
Western Europe	5.2	3.3	2.9	123
Oceania	4.0	3.3	2.7	9
Canada	3.0	2.6	2.3	11
Japan	12.0	4.9	4.3	28
South Africa	12	12	11	3
Eastern Europe	36	12	11	15
Latin America	38	18	16	24
Soviet Union	147	32	24	12
Asia[1]	196	95	65	11
Africa[2]	191	111	112	5
India	902	718	515	1.5
China	27,707	18,673	2,022	0.5
World	18	14	13	375

[1]Excluding Japan, China, India.
[2]Excluding South Africa.

Source: Worldwatch Institute, based on Motor Vehicle Manufacturers Association, *Facts and Figures* (Detroit, Mich.: various editions).

twice the world average. Long waiting lists indicate that there is still enormous pent-up demand. Access to car ownership remains regulated by bureaucratic allocation and heavy taxation.[11]

Charting the automobile's future in these countries is an uncertain undertaking. On the one hand, General Secretary Gorbachev's attempts at perestroika, the restructuring of the Soviet economy, may well lead to a stronger emphasis on consumer goods, with the automobile near the top of the list. In much of Eastern Europe, on the other hand, the unresolved debt crisis may keep a lid on expansion of car ownership.

Many developing countries are rapidly adopting the automobile. Governments are anxious to encourage the development of auto-centered transportation systems because they consider the car indispensable as an engine of economic growth and as a cornerstone of industrial development. They are importing fully assembled vehicles, inviting multinational car companies to set up assembly plants, or attempting to build their own domestic motor industries. Car ownership in the Third World has risen sharply, averaging an annual growth rate of 11 percent in the first half of the seventies and 8 percent in the second half. Even though Third World fleets still grow twice as fast as those in the industrial world, the global economic crisis clearly put the brakes on. Only the developing nations of Asia, unencumbered by the debt problems besetting Latin America and Africa, further quickened the pace.[12]

With only a few exceptions, car ownership in the Third World is unlikely to reach the scale existing in industrial countries. At average per capita incomes of below $2,000 in Latin America, below $1,500 in the Far East, and below $500 in sub-Saharan Africa and South Asia, buying and maintaining a car is simply beyond the reach of the overwhelming majority of people. The highly skewed wealth distribution patterns in most countries may foster a small, privileged class with ample purchasing power, but they effectively limit the number of potential car owners.[13]

China and India together account for 38 percent of the world's population, but they own scarcely one-half of 1 percent of its automobiles. Until the late seventies, these governments assigned cars one of the lowest development priorities. Both, however, have since embarked on policies that seek to emulate the motorized transport systems of the industrial West. The number of cars in China has risen tenfold, to a half million, and is likely to keep increasing as wealth distribution becomes less egalitarian.[14]

Government forecasts predict a fleet of 4 million in China by 2000. In a bid to reduce costly imports, the government wants to raise domestic car output—in joint ventures with foreign firms—from 20,000 in 1987 to as much as 1 million annually by the end of the century. To meet this production goal, China needs to invest more than $10 billion in its motor industry. Similarly, India's car production has shot up fourfold since 1980, to 115,000 vehicles in 1986; in the nineties, it may produce a quarter-million autos annually.[15]

Third World car ownership is concentrated mainly in the newly industrializing countries of Latin America and Southeast Asia, and in the major oil-exporting countries whose appetites for cars were whetted by soaring oil revenues in the seventies and low gasoline retail prices. Argentina, Brazil, and Mexico together account for almost half the cars in the developing world. During the first half of the seventies, their car markets grew at a phenomenal 16 percent per year, and Brazil became the world's ninth largest producer.[16]

Yet the emergence of the debt crisis in 1982, coming on the heels of surging oil prices in the seventies, shattered the auto industry's expectations that the bulk of future growth would occur in Latin America. The debt crunch compelled these nations to marshal their financial resources for debt servicing, precipitating major recessions. In 1986, debt-service payments absorbed one-quarter of Brazil's export earnings, and almost half of Mexico's and Argentina's. Soaring interest rates and falling real wages eroded purchasing power and considerably shrank the number of potential car buyers.[17]

Car purchases in Argentina, Brazil, and Mexico fell by half in the eighties, and the once dynamic Brazilian auto industry stumbled from boom to bust and back. But the debt crunch did not diminish the commitment to an auto-centered transportation system. To make cars more affordable, the Mexican government in November 1984 required that 25 percent of domestic auto production be stripped-down "austerity" models.[18]

Brazil and Mexico embraced automobile exports as an avenue to escape the debt morass. First encouraged by generous government

"The debt crisis in 1982
shattered
the auto industry's expectations
that the bulk of future growth
would occur in Latin America."

incentives in 1972 to pay for ballooning oil imports, exports now account for a rising share of Brazil's car production. Vehicles slated for export even get first claim on scarce auto parts. In 1987, when domestic demand collapsed, foreign sales soared to 40 percent. In Mexico, the share of production sold abroad has grown from less than 5 percent in 1982 to 20 percent in 1985, making cars the country's second largest revenue earner after oil.[19]

15

Now India, Indonesia, Malaysia, Taiwan, and Thailand are gearing up to join Brazil and Mexico—plus Japan, various European countries, South Korea, and the Soviet Union—in a fight for a slice of the export market. The enormous size of the U.S. market makes it the primary target for exporters. Despite relatively low growth rates, the volume of new-car purchases still surpasses that of any other single market. Between 1970 and 1985, the United States added as many cars to its roads as the entire Third World now possesses. The U.S. Commerce Department expects imports to capture 36 percent of the American market in 1988.[20]

Whether these export strategies will bear fruit is questionable. Slow demand growth, surplus production capacities, and rising protectionism make it unlikely that all exporters can find buyers. At the same time that these manufacturers expose themselves to the vagaries of the global car market and the dangers of protectionism, the low wage rates on which their export strategies hinge inhibit the emergence of a viable domestic market.

South Korea epitomizes this dilemma. The government encouraged the buildup of an indigenous car industry through favorable tax, credit, and export assistance policies. Since the early seventies, South Korea's annual output has grown fiftyfold, to over 700,000 units in 1987, and it has emerged as a serious challenger to Japan's dominance in the small-car market segment. But car ownership at home has been hobbled through high taxes on car purchases, registration, and gasoline and through low wages. Exports have claimed a steadily rising share of production, accounting for 57 percent in 1986 and an estimated 75 percent in 1987.[21]

Domestic car sales in South Korea tripled between 1980 and 1985, but there is still only one car for every 77 people. In the wake of widespread strikes and political unrest in the summer of 1987, the Korean car industry may gradually have to adjust its competitive strategy: Higher labor costs may curb its export drive but could assure the growth of a middle class at home who can afford to own a car.[22]

The overwhelming majority of the Third World's population can never aspire to such a goal. The promotion of car ownership thus entails sharp inequities: The resources of poor and wealthy alike are drained, though only a few enjoy the benefits. It is questionable whether "democratization" of car ownership—if it could be achieved—can be considered desirable. Mass motorization in the western industrial countries is leading to depleted oil reserves, impaired human health, and a degraded environment, as discussed in the following sections. If a repetition of these mistakes on a global basis is to be avoided, industrial and developing nations need to curb their reliance on automobiles and join together in a search for more sustainable alternatives.

Depending More on Oil, Searching for Alternatives

Because cars run almost exclusively on petroleum-based fuels, the auto industry is sensitive to changes in the price and availability of oil. As a means of transportation, the automobile is, after all, only as reliable as its fuel supplies. Since the first oil crisis, other sectors of the economy have reduced their reliance on petroleum. But no easy substitutes are available for automotive fuels. Thus, automobiles now account for a larger portion of oil demand than they did at the time of the first oil crisis. Since 1976, the United States has used more petroleum each year for transportation purposes than it has produced. In 1985, the transport sector consumed 63 percent of all oil used in the United States (up from 50 percent in 1973), 44 percent of petroleum used in Western Europe, 35 percent in Japan, and 49 percent in developing countries.[23]

Australian researchers Peter Newman and Jeffrey Kenworthy surveyed 32 cities in Asia, Australia, North America, and Western Europe. They found that, on average, people in the highly car-oriented American cities use twice as much gasoline per capita as in Australian cities, four times as much as in European cities, and ten times as much as in Asian cities. Even if adjusted for the higher personal incomes, lower gasoline prices, and less efficient vehicles prevalent in the United States, gasoline consumption in the other cities would still be considerably lower. U.S. cars travel some 1,250 billion miles annually—almost the same distance as all other cars worldwide taken together.[24] (See Table 4.)

17

Table 4: World Automobile Travel, Selected Countries, Circa 1985

Country	Distance Traveled (million vehicle miles)	Distance per Car (miles)
United States	1,253,248	9,801
West Germany	194,621	8,446
Japan	164,625	5,913
France	162,702	7,763
United Kingdom	141,588	8,073
Italy	132,610	6,148
Australia[1]	59,684	9,501
Spain	34,962	5,651
Sweden	32,851	7,452
Argentina	19,350	7,063
Poland	12,540	3,416
South Korea	3,119	5,603
Indonesia[1]	2,360	3,726
Cameroon	570	7,867[2]
Rwanda	176	9,315

[1]1982.
[2]1983.

Source: International Road Federation, *World Road Statistics 1981-1985* (Washington, D.C.: 1986).

The oil crises of the seventies reinforced the notion that a transportation system centered on the private passenger car can impose tremendous costs on society, whether in the form of escalating fuel import bills or huge expenditures of capital and resources to tap domestic fuel sources. Higher prices made oil account for a rapidly growing share of total imports of most countries. (See Table 5.) The average fraction of Third World export earnings used to pay for oil imports tripled during the seventies. By 1981, Brazil spent over half its export

Table 5: Value of Oil Imports as Share of Total Imports, Selected Countries, 1970–86

Country	1970	1975	1981–83[1]	1986
		(percent)		
Brazil	11	24	53	43[2]
Turkey	8	17	48	n.a.
Yugoslavia	4	10	23	26[3]
India[4]	6	18	41	20[3]
Japan	15	36	41	19
Kenya[4]	7	24	34	15
Spain[4]	11	22	33	14
Morocco[4]	3	9	25	13
Poland	n.a.	5	12	12
South Korea	6	17	25	11
United States	6	25	29	10
West Germany	8	16	19	10
Thailand[4]	4	18	23	9
Bangladesh	n.a.	7	19	8

[1]Peak year for 1981–83 period.
[2]1985.
[3]1984.
[4]Crude oil imports only.

Source: Worldwatch Institute, based upon International Monetary Fund, *International Financial Statistics Yearbook 1987* (Washington, D.C.: 1987).

earnings to pay for imported oil. Kenya, South Korea, and Thailand spent close to one-third, and Bangladesh, two-thirds.[25]

Brazil, by far the Third World's largest car market and oil importer, saw its oil bill skyrocket from $280 million in 1970 to $10.3 billion in 1980. Higher domestic oil production and a controversial program to generate ethanol fuel from sugar crops allowed the country to cut its reliance on imported oil by 60 percent between 1979 and 1986. Yet, providing the fuel from domestic sources carried a hefty price tag, requiring large-scale investment and government subsidies. The Brazilian government has spent an estimated $8 billion to prop up the country's ethanol industry alone. As international oil prices collapsed, subsidies grew from $650 million in 1985 to $2 billion in 1986.[26]

The dark clouds cast over the auto's future by the two oil shocks in the seventies seemed to recede in the eighties. Car sales quickly resumed growth as concern over oil prices and supplies faded from memory. Cheaper gasoline served as a catalyst for increased and faster driving and removed an incentive for purchasing more fuel-efficient cars. Edging upward again since 1983, global gasoline consumption surpassed its 1978 peak in 1986. (See Figure 2.) Unless car fuel efficiency is boosted further to offset these trends, gasoline consumption will continue to rise. Growing demand will eventually put increased pressure on production capacities.[27]

Large surplus oil production capacities make it unlikely that another major crisis will be triggered soon by unforeseen events. But the discrepancy between regional production levels and productive capacities means that countries are bound to rely increasingly on oil imports from the Middle East. Countries outside the Organization of Petroleum Exporting Countries (OPEC) are pumping oil at record rates, but most of them are unlikely to sustain current production levels for many years. Non-OPEC oil fields now supply as much as 68 percent of global production, yet account for only 32 percent of the world's proven oil reserves. By contrast, the spigot has been tightened on OPEC's prolific oil fields. The Middle East alone contains well over half of global reserves and has by far the lowest production costs.[28]

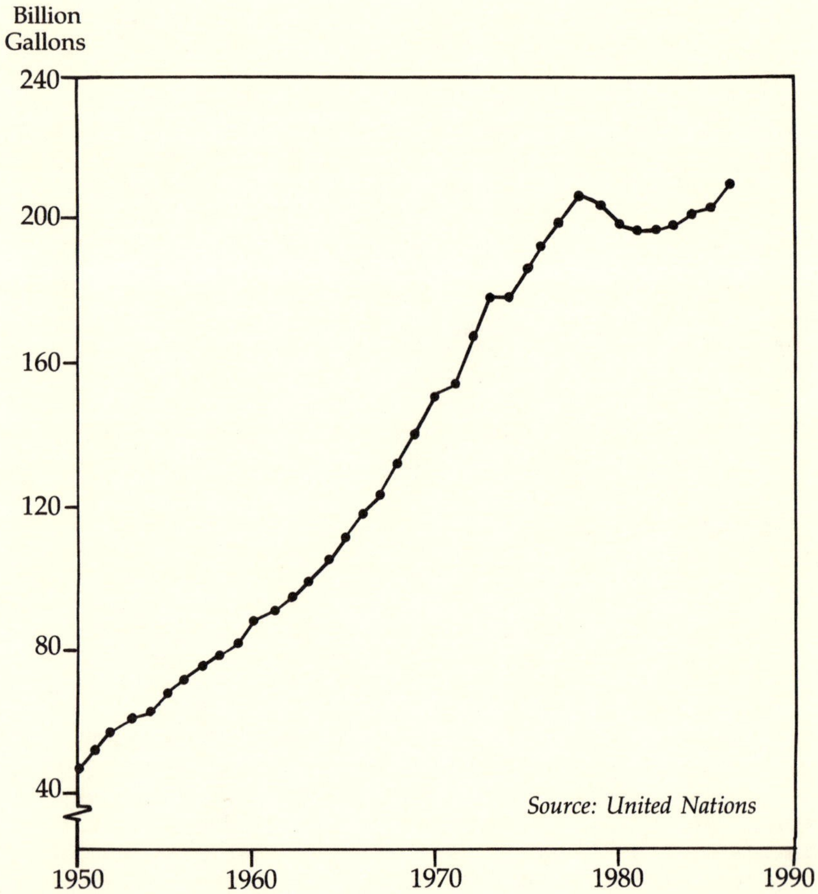
Billion
Gallons
240
200
160
120
80
40
Source: United Nations
1950
1960
1970
1980
1990

Figure 2: World Passenger Car Gasoline Consumption, 1950–86

"Worldwide proven reserves
have grown modestly,
providing a
resource base for
just over 32 years."

The United States, already the world's largest oil importer, is rapidly increasing its reliance on foreign petroleum. Domestic reserves are now well on their way toward depletion, and production costs are among the highest in the world. U.S. output dropped in 1986 and 1987, while imports increased 30 percent and now account for 40 percent of national consumption. A continuation of these trends will put a growing strain on world oil markets. Greater pressure on world markets will also come from developing countries, which keep increasing their reliance on petroleum in transportation and other sectors of the economy.[29]

Despite record exploration expenditures in the seventies, worldwide proven oil reserves have grown only modestly, providing a resource base for just over 32 years at current production rates. The search for oil has been concentrated in the United States, where costs are high and yields low. Even though fairly large areas around the globe remain comparatively little explored, geologists agree that new, yet-to-be discovered oil deposits will be much smaller than the giant fields of the past; they will thus be harder to come by and costlier to develop. The worldwide cost of adding a barrel of new productive capacity from 1973 to 1983 was 23 times higher than in the preceding decade.[30]

Rising oil prices in the seventies spurred the search for alternatives to petroleum-based fuels. Proposals spanned a wide spectrum of options, including grandiose but ill-fated schemes to crash-develop a massive oil-shale and coal-based synthetic fuels industry. Providing alternative fuels in sufficient quantity proved to be prohibitively expensive, hampered by technical immaturity, and environmentally damaging.

Since the peak of the second oil crisis, alternative fuels have been a dormant issue. Interest in them has been recently revived, however, by warnings of a renewed oil crisis and concerns about the environmental effects of gasoline use. Attention currently centers on alcohol fuels (ethanol and methanol), natural gas, and, to a lesser degree, electricity. Alcohol fuels can be derived from agricultural waste and other biomass sources; methanol can also be produced from natural gas and coal.

Brazil's *Proalcool* program is widely regarded the "success story" of the ethanol industry. Sugarcane-derived ethanol provided roughly half the country's automotive fuel in 1986. When the program was launched in 1975, the goal was to have all cars running on an 80/20 gasoline-ethanol blend. Since the second oil crisis, however, an attempt has been made to reduce the gasoline proportion further. Indeed, almost one-third of Brazilian cars are now capable of running on pure ethanol.[31]

The scope of Brazil's program, however, may not be readily replicable elsewhere, because of either insufficient crop surpluses, or a lack of government commitment, or an automotive fleet that is simply too large. Even the most optimistic forecasts do not foresee a large-scale shift toward biomass-produced alcohol fuels in the major automobile-owning societies. The United States, the world's second largest ethanol producer, currently covers less than 1 percent of its gasoline consumption with that fuel.

If corn were used as a feedstock, almost 40 percent of the entire U.S. annual harvest would have to be earmarked for ethanol production in order to meet 10 percent of the nation's automotive fuel demand. The 1987 grain surplus of the European Economic Community (EEC) would yield enough ethanol for about 5 percent of current gasoline demand among its members.[32]

Sugar beets and, where it can be cultivated, sugarcane are more efficient in converting sunlight into stored energy, and therefore promise greater fuel yields than corn and other grains. But in most of the heavily auto-dependent countries, the production of alcohol fuels would still require large inputs of agricultural land. Thus, transportation fuel needs could come in conflict with food requirements, particularly if both of them keep growing.

Coal and natural gas reserves are plentiful enough to produce methanol on a large scale in resource-rich countries. For the United States, coal is an option, while domestic gas deposits appear insufficient to sustain a methanol-fueled future for the transport sector. Abundant as these sources may be, however, ultimately they are as finite as petroleum. And coal's use on a large scale has serious implications for the trend toward global warming, as discussed in the section on reducing emissions.

A major drawback of all alcohol fuels is that some 30-40 percent of the original energy content of their potential feedstocks (biomass, coal, and natural gas) is lost in the conversion process. Numerous studies suggest that the total amount of energy inputs to obtain ethanol—including energy required to fuel farmers' vehicles, to produce fertilizer and pesticides, and to ferment and purify the alcohol—may be close to or even surpass the eventual energy output. A host of new approaches to the distillation process are under study, such as continuous fermentation techniques, new yeasts and enzymes, and the use of solar energy. These may one day boost the efficiency of alcohol fuel production.[33]

Using natural gas directly as an automotive fuel, either in compressed (CNG) or in liquefied form (LPG), appears more practical than tapping it as a feedstock for alcohol fuels because less of the original energy is lost in the conversion process. Today, there are more than 300,000 CNG vehicles on the road in Italy; the Soviet Union plans to fuel over 1 million such cars by 1990; and Argentina, Australia, Brazil, Indonesia, Malaysia, New Zealand, Pakistan, and Thailand are beginning to use natural gas as a transportation fuel. Japan and Italy meet almost 4 percent of their national transportation fuel demand with LPG.[34]

In the more distant future, hydrogen—the most common element in the universe—may become a widely used fuel, in either liquid or compressed gaseous form. Hydrogen can be generated from coal, natural gas, or oil, but for environmental and supply reasons the most desirable path is to produce it from water (through electrolysis, a process that uses electricity to split the water into hydrogen and oxygen). A number of new technologies to produce hydrogen are under investigation; for example, construction is to begin this year on the world's first experimental solar-hydrogen plant in Bavaria, West Germany. Cost is still a major impediment to commercialization, and vehicle technology has not yet advanced beyond the prototype stage. Canada, Japan, and West Germany have made major commitments to promote hydrogen research and development. In the United States, however, hydrogen has yet to attract R&D funding commensurate with its enormous potential.[35]

Because hydrogen-powered vehicles will not be available in the near future, an intermediate fuel may well be needed or desired. Technically the simplest transition would be from CNG to high-pressure gaseous hydrogen vehicles. One advantage of this approach is that distribution and storage systems (including a vehicle's fuel tank) of CNG and hydrogen vehicles are likely to be relatively similar.

Electric vehicles promise higher energy efficiency and quieter operation than conventional internal combustion engines. Barring major breakthroughs in battery technology and cost, however, electric vehicles will likely be confined to market niches where performance and range criteria are less important than in the overall passenger car market. Moreover, such vehicles can only be a viable alternative if the fuels used in electricity generation are renewable. Fuel cells could some day hold the key to making electric vehicles more acceptable. A fuel cell converts the chemical energy in hydrogen, methanol, and natural gas directly into electrical energy without mechanical losses. It runs best and most economically on pure hydrogen. But its commercial appeal remains a matter of controversy.[36]

Alternative fuels have to overcome considerable odds if they are to make more than just a dent in the motor fuel market. The most daunting obstacle is usually referred to as the "chicken and egg" dilemma: an infrastructure—fuels, vehicles, service stations—will not spring up unless there is adequate demand, while such demand is unlikely to materialize in the absence of adequate infrastructure. Fuel blends that contain more than 20 percent alcohol fuel cannot be used in conventional engines without some modification. "Fuel-flexible" vehicles, running either on gasoline or alternative fuels, could alleviate that problem, at least in a transitional phase. But they may be more cumbersome to operate and they are less efficient than vehicles designed for a single fuel. Vehicles powered by natural gas, hydrogen, or electricity also still suffer from unresolved technical problems, which may preclude consumer acceptance. Fuel tanks or batteries are likely to be heavier and bulkier, and therefore impose stricter limits on vehicle range.[37]

Except for natural gas vehicles, cost has been another handicap in adopting alternative fuels. Studies recently commissioned by the European Parliament and the U.S. Department of Agriculture estimate, respectively, that a barrel of oil would have to cost $40 or $67 to make ethanol competitive with gasoline. Methanol is closer to being competitive, particularly when made from natural gas. Hydrogen costs are almost certain to decrease with a greater R&D effort.[38]

It is not clear, however, just how meaningful such figures are. Fluctuating prices for oil, natural gas, coal, and agricultural crops frustrate efforts to make sound cost comparisons between gasoline and competing fuels. Moreover, oil prices do not reflect the real cost to society. They take into account neither the finite character of petroleum reserves nor the health and environmental burdens associated with the production and consumption of gasoline. Finally, it may well be worth paying a premium for supply security.

The potential of alternative fuels to substitute for gasoline varies considerably from country to country and fuel to fuel. In the short run, no single alternative is likely to become a panacea with global applicability. Those that emerge are likely to supplement gasoline, rather than replace it. In the longer run, hydrogen could become a universally used fuel. But an enormous research boost is needed now to make its generation less costly and to achieve breakthroughs in hydrogen-vehicle technology.

As Brazil has shown, governments can play a key role in laying the groundwork for an alternative fuels market. Laws that set tough but reasonable goals for the gradual replacement of gasoline and provide incentives to meet such goals can help overcome the "chicken and egg" problem.

Enhancing Fuel Efficiency

26 After the first oil crisis, car companies around the world made dramatic strides to boost fuel efficiency. Until the early eighties, efficiency improved sharply year after year. This was particularly true in the United States, where the industry was subject to the triple pressure of rising fuel costs, intense Japanese competition, and mandatory U.S. government standards (effective in 1978). New passenger cars in the United States today are almost twice as efficient as the gas-guzzling behemoths of the early seventies; as a result, the average fleet fuel economy rose from 13 miles per gallon (MPG) in 1973 to 18 MPG in 1986. (See Figure 3.) Had fuel efficiency stayed at the dismal level of the early seventies, U.S. gasoline consumption would have grown by fully one-third and pressure on world oil markets would be much greater today. Instead, consumption remains approximately the same as 15 years ago.[39]

Despite these gains, American-made cars continue to trail those produced elsewhere. New U.S. cars travel an average of 27 miles per gallon; their European and Japanese competitors achieve roughly 30 MPG. The U.S. average fleet efficiency of 18 MPG also compares poorly with the mid-twenties range of other industrial countries. Due to lower efficiency and more driving, the average North American car still burns up more than twice as much gasoline each year as its counterpart in Japan or Western Europe. (See Table 6.) Annual gasoline consumption per car among countries in the Organisation for Economic Co-operation and Development (OECD) fell by one-quarter between 1973 and 1985. During that same period, the OECD fleet expanded by 45 percent, but its total fuel consumption grew only by 4 percent.[40]

Fuel economy in the Soviet Union and East Germany is roughly on a par with Europe. Brazil lags behind Europe and Japan, but is ahead of the United States. Comparatively little information is available on fuel efficiency in other developing countries. Most cars on the road in the Third World are either imported or engineered and designed by western car manufacturers. However, because on average they rely on

Miles Per
Gallon

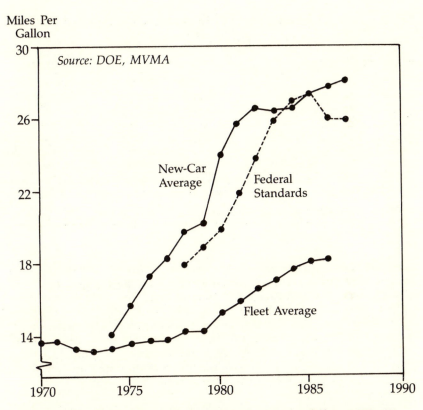

Figure 3: Fuel Consumption of U.S. Automobiles, 1970–87

older designs and because maintenance is often poor, the Third World's automobiles are likely to be less efficient than those in industrial countries.[41]

Once the world had passed the peak of the second oil crisis, fuel economy goals swiftly lost their urgency. Since 1983, gains in fuel economy in the United States and most other OECD members have

Table 6: Annual Gasoline Use in Passenger Cars, Selected Regions, 1973–85

Region or Country	1973	1985	Change
	(gallons per car)		(percent)
North America	1,000	786	-21
Japan	473	345	-27
Australia	701	528	-25
Western Europe[1]	399	317	-21
OECD[1]	757	568	-25

[1]Excluding France.

Source: International Energy Agency, *Energy Policies and Programmes of IEA Countries, 1986 Review* (Paris: Organisation for Economic Co-operation and Development, 1987).

fallen short of the impressive achievements between 1974 and 1982. In the United States, gains in reducing car weight and engine displacement leveled off abruptly after 1980-81, and the changeover from eight to four cylinders stalled. Since 1983, Ford and General Motors (GM) have consistently failed to meet government standards. Lending the official seal to this, the Reagan administration reduced the federally mandated fuel economy standards from 27.5 to 26 MPG in 1986. The following year, the average fuel economy for new U.S.-built cars slipped slightly below the 1986 average.[42]

Moreover, the rising popularity of light trucks limits the potential for future efficiency gains. Even though light trucks posted some efficiency gains, they remain one-third less fuel-efficient than new U.S. passenger cars; their total gasoline consumption more than doubled between 1970 and 1985. At the same time, the earlier fuel efficiency improvements in Europe and Japan have been partly offset by consumers' growing preference for larger and more powerful vehicles.[43]

But the world could make much greater strides toward fuel efficiency. Improved fuel economy is crucial when the global car fleet and the

"Raising automotive fuel efficiency
still offers a good chance
to minimize the impact
of the next oil crisis."

number of miles traveled keep increasing. Between 1976 and 1985, for example, the miles driven in passenger cars worldwide rose by about 50 percent.[44]

Although technical solutions seem almost invariably to generate the greatest excitement and attention, simple human adjustments could double efficiency virtually overnight. For example, even a highly fuel-efficient car is inefficiently used when it carries only the driver, as is the case for over half the auto trips made in the United States; 87 percent of all trips have at most two passengers. Car pooling and ride-sharing are still in their infancy compared with their potential. In 1984, the amount of energy used by U.S. cars for every passenger-mile of travel was just as high as back in 1971.[45]

Because technical opportunities are far from exhausted, raising auto-motive fuel efficiency still offers a good chance to minimize the impact of the next oil crisis. Today, the world's cars average 20–25 miles on a gallon of gasoline. Doubling that could save some 10 percent of the world's current oil consumption.[46]

A myriad of factors determine a vehicle's fuel use. Weight reduction and improvements in engine and transmission efficiency hold the greatest promise. In addition, aerodynamics, tire rolling resistance, the energy dissipation of the brakes, and the energy consumption of accessories merit further improvement.[47]

On average, a 10-percent weight reduction will yield a 6-percent fuel economy gain. Past fuel economy improvements in the United States have primarily been accomplished through lowered weights and shifts to front-wheel drive. Only 10-15 percent of the gains came from a shift to smaller cars. Fuel efficiency has thus not come at the expense of reduced car-interior space. The average weight of American cars has dropped from 4,000 pounds to 3,000 over the past decade, but is still considerably heavier than that of Japanese and European models. Further gains will likely result from greater substitution of lighter-weight materials for the steel and cast-iron components of today's vehicles.[48]

The new materials, in order of their potential contribution to lighter cars, include magnesium, plastics, aluminum, and high-strength low-alloy steel; without any sacrifice of strength (and therefore safety), they offer weight losses of between 23 and 75 percent. And they now promise heat and stress resistance and design flexibility comparable to conventional materials.[49]

The extra cost per pound of weight saved has emerged as an important component in fuel efficiency economics. If higher raw material expenses for these lightweight materials can be offset by considerably lower fabrication and assembly costs, their use is attractive. Also, higher energy requirements for their manufacture are usually more than balanced by the energy gains realized over the lifetime of a vehicle.[50]

Plastics have exhibited the most dramatic growth of all new automotive materials. In 1985, 8-11 percent of the vehicle weight of cars manufactured in Japan, the United States, and West Germany was accounted for by plastics; that share could grow to 18-20 percent early next century, as structural and load-bearing components made of composite materials are developed.[51]

Toyota leads in the use of low-alloy steel; the company's average car now incorporates more than 300 pounds. The typical U.S. 1985 model, by contrast, used just over 200 pounds. Due to higher cost, the use of aluminum has grown less rapidly than that of other materials. Applications are focused on heat exchangers and wheels, and increasingly on cylinder heads and transmission cases. Magnesium is the lightest material, but its use is expected to grow the slowest, due to its high cost, flammability, and tendency to corrode. It accounts for less than 1 percent of the weight of most new cars.[52]

Reducing the weight of a car allows the use of smaller engines without having to sacrifice performance. Engine efficiency can also be improved by varying the number of cylinders operating at any given time, running the motor at more optimal loads, minimizing energy loss through exhaust gases, and improving fuel combustion (for ex-

"Reducing
the weight of a car
allows the use of smaller engines
without having to sacrifice
performance."

ample, through leaner air-to-fuel mixtures). Reducing engine warm-up time is another important goal since fuel efficiency can drop by half when an engine is cold. Potential fuel economy gains from these approaches range from 5 to 20 percent.[53]

Advanced engine designs such as the adiabatic diesel (which minimizes heat loss) and the stratified-charge engine (which features a "rich" air-to-fuel mixture surrounding the spark plug while maintaining an efficient and cleaner-burning overall lean mixture) promise fuel economy improvements of 25-40 percent. While American automakers have been reluctant to make firm commitments to such engine designs, Honda's CVCC has used a stratified-charge engine commercially for a number of years. And Toyota is said to have developed a stratified-charge lean-burn engine with commercial application.[54]

Increases in the number of gears allow a motor to run at its most efficient speed. Continuously variable transmissions (CVTs) essentially give a car an unlimited number of gears; they offer fuel savings of 20-24 percent, particularly in urban, stop-and-go, driving. However, the higher torque (to drive the engine shaft) and power demands of larger-sized cars surpass the capabilities of current-generation CVTs. These will have to be met by technology now under development. Japan's Subaru, in its Justy subcompact model, was the first to introduce CVT technology commercially. Italy's Fiat has just begun offering the CVT in its Uno model, and Ford Europe's Fiesta will follow shortly.[55]

Energy losses due to braking and idling—which occur frequently during urban driving—can amount to as much as one-third of a vehicle's original kinetic energy. Energy storage systems—such as a flywheel device—together with a CVT can alleviate this problem by capturing an engine's excess power whenever the driving requirements are less than its output. This power can then be tapped at some other time, thereby enabling smaller engines than in today's models. Researchers at the University of Wisconsin hope to double fuel economy with such a system.[56]

Reducing aerodynamic drag becomes more important as driving speeds increase, and is therefore of particular interest in Europe, where motorists drive much faster than elsewhere. Aerodynamic drag quadruples when a car's speed doubles. Generally, cutting the drag of a vehicle by 10 percent will drop its highway fuel consumption by 5-6 percent and its urban fuel consumption by 2-3 percent.[57]

Lowering tire rolling resistance by 10 percent improves fuel economy by 3-4 percent. Improvements in this regard, which have been achieved primarily by reducing the amount of tire surface in contact with the road, are limited by comfort and safety considerations. The focus is now on new tire materials and processing methods. In addition, optimizing tire pressure can yield fuel economy gains and reduce tire wear while increasing safety.[58]

The most efficient cars currently available are about twice as efficient as the average new car on the road. At the top of the list is a Japanese model, the Suzuki Sprint, which gets 57 MPG. More advanced prototypes, such as the Peugeot ECO 2000, Volkswagen E80, and Toyota AXV, achieve anywhere from 70 to over 100 MPG; Sweden's Volvo claims its LCP 2000, which contains more lightweight materials than any other car, will achieve a fuel efficiency in excess of 100 MPG without sacrificing performance, size, safety, or emissions criteria. Renault's VESTA scored a stunning 124 MPG in prototype testing.[59]

The prospects that innovations currently on the drawing boards or tested in prototypes will be commercialized in a timely fashion are not encouraging, however. Car companies around the world have responded to lower oil prices by scaling down research and development programs and, more importantly, by slowing down their efforts to incorporate advanced fuel economy technologies in mass-produced cars. Instead, consumers are offered styling changes and gadgetry.

Volvo, for example, has no plans to market the LCP 2000, even though it seems ready for mass production. Peugeot, meanwhile, refers to the ECO 2000 as its "crisis car"—to be held in reserve should another oil crisis materialize. But lead times are too long to permit a rapid introduction of more fuel-efficient models should the fortunes on the world oil market change. It takes three to five years to retool and bring a new car model into production, and another 10 years or more for it to fully replace its less efficient predecessors on the road.

High expectations for GM's Saturn, Ford's Alpha, and Chrysler's Liberty small-car models have not been met, as the companies either reconfigured the cars as bigger models or abandoned plans to put them into production. Indeed, one industry analyst joked that GM's Saturn project was at the "leading edge of old technology." In keeping with Henry Ford II's 1971 dictum that "mini-cars mean mini-profits," General Motors and Ford—and increasingly Chrysler as well—prefer to concentrate on big cars, where profit margins are large. In the small-car segment, all three U.S. companies increasingly rely on "sponsored" imports—marketing cars often designed, engineered, or manufactured abroad. As a result, they could find themselves without a sufficient manufacturing base to meet the demand for smaller cars when it develops again.[60]

In the seventies, the United States held a research lead in advanced fuel efficiency projects such as energy storage systems and the lean-burn engine. But with the advent of the oil glut, the American car companies abandoned fuel economy as a strategic goal. At the same time, U.S. government support for fuel economy R&D was terminated or reduced by the Reagan administration.

Today, the Japanese and Europeans are the pacesetters in the quest for higher fuel efficiency. Toyota and Honda lead the development of lean-burn motors, Japanese firms are most advanced in ceramic engine development, and European firms are strong contenders in energy storage systems. Even in aerodynamics, where American companies are still ahead, a research lead has not translated into practical advances.

One reason auto companies lag in commercializing highly fuel-efficient technologies is the current lack of consumer interest. Improved fuel economy is of little concern when gasoline claims a relatively small share of the overall cost of operating a car. In 1986, gasoline and

34

motor oil accounted for only 15 percent of total operating costs per mile in the United States, down from 26 percent in 1975. Soaring insurance costs and maintenance expenditures have replaced fuel costs as the main concern.[61]

Beyond a certain point, consumer interest in higher fuel economy wanes as each increment yields proportionally smaller savings. At current U.S. fuel prices, for someone driving 10,000 miles a year, an improvement from 10 to 20 MPG will save $500 annually; but doubling that to 40 MPG promises "only" an additional savings of $250, and doubling again, a comparatively meager $125.

Gasoline taxes are widely used as instruments to shape drivers' behavior. In general, oil-exporting countries have kept domestic gasoline retail prices well below world market price levels, while importers have traditionally imposed taxes to restrain consumption and thus heavy reliance on imported supplies. South Korea, for example, charges its domestic consumers three-and-a-half times as much as it costs the country to import gasoline. Venezuela, by contrast, keeps its retail prices to three-quarters of the international price. The United States is one of very few oil-importing countries to keep gasoline taxes low.[62]

High fuel taxes, collected per unit of consumption, have had some success in restraining gasoline consumption. But they have affected driving patterns more than they have steered consumers toward the most efficient cars. For example, even though fuel prices in Western Europe are roughly twice as high as those in the United States, the efficiency savings are not of the same magnitude. A tax that is levied on the sale of a new vehicle could shape consumers' purchasing decisions if it were tailored to a vehicle's fuel economy.[63]

The major barrier to higher fuel economy is not technological but political: How can corporations and motorists be persuaded to produce and use less fuel-thirsty vehicles? Left to their own devices, both industry and consumers will enjoy the free ride afforded by low fuel prices and will neglect fuel economy. Governments need to adopt a strong framework—a set of new standards and taxes—to boost fuel

"Left to their own devices,
industry and consumers
will enjoy the free ride
afforded by lower fuel prices
and will neglect fuel economy."

efficiency. Given the range of advanced fuel economy technologies now installed in prototypes, on the shelf, or on a drawing board, striving for 40-50 MPG for new cars by the end of the century is a reasonable goal.

35

Reducing Emissions

The most alarming effect of mass motorization may not be the depletion of fossil fuels but the large-scale damage to human health and the natural environment. Researchers at the University of California estimate that the use of gasoline and diesel fuel in the United States alone may cause up to 30,000 deaths every year. And the American Lung Association estimates that air pollution from motor vehicles, power plants, and industrial fuel combustion costs the United States $40 billion annually in health care and lost productivity.[64]

An internal combustion engine produces numerous air pollutants. Those that are currently regulated in most industrial countries include lead, carbon monoxide, nitrogen and sulfur oxides, particulate matter, and volatile organic compounds (consisting mostly of unburned hydrocarbons). Among the unregulated pollutants are carbon dioxide (CO_2), benzene (a human carcinogen), toluene, xylene, and ethylene dibromide. In addition, vapors escaping from unburnt gasoline are toxic air pollutants.

Cars, trucks, and buses play a prominent role in generating virtually all the major air pollutants, especially in cities. In OECD member countries, they contribute 75 percent of carbon monoxide emissions, 48 percent of nitrogen oxides, 40 percent of hydrocarbons, 13 percent of particulates, and 3 percent of sulfur oxides. Worldwide, the production and use of automotive fuels account for an estimated 17 percent of all carbon dioxide released from fossil fuels. Transportation is also the primary source of lead pollution. The adverse health effects of these pollutants are fairly well established.[65]

Perhaps the best known and most pervasive synergistic effect of these pollutants is photochemical smog—the brown haze that causes such health disorders as bronchial diseases and lung damage, dramatically restricts visibility, and erodes buildings and monuments. Ozone—the most important component of smog—is the product of complex reactions between nitrogen oxides and hydrocarbons in the presence of sunlight. It has also been strongly implicated in central Europe's "Waldsterben," the massive damage afflicting forests. And the U.S. National Crop Loss Assessment Program found that damage from ozone results in annual yield losses of $1.9 billion to $4.5 billion for four cash crops—corn, wheat, soybeans, and peanuts.[66]

In 1986, between 40 million and 75 million Americans were living in areas that failed to attain National Ambient Air Quality Standards for ozone, carbon monoxide, and particulates. If these same standards were in force elsewhere, they would routinely be exceeded in many cities. The carbon monoxide content of the air in Budapest, for instance, is two-and-a-half times the permissible level in Hungary; smog in Athens is reckoned to claim as many as six lives a day. São Paulo, Mexico City, Cairo, and New Delhi are among the cities with the world's worst air pollution problems. In Calcutta, an estimated 60 percent of residents are believed to suffer from respiratory diseases related to air pollution.[67]

Although the role of automotive emissions in urban air pollution has been extensively studied, their contribution to the phenomenon commonly known as acid rain has received comparatively scant attention. Nitrogen and sulfur oxides, together with unburnt hydrocarbons, are the principal components of the acid precipitation that is destroying freshwater aquatic life and forests throughout central Europe and North America. A recent study by the Environmental Defense Fund suggests that nitrogen oxides in acid rain also play a role in the degradation of marine life in Atlantic coastal waters. Airborne nitrates stimulate excessive algae growth, the decomposition of which chokes off the oxygen supply and blocks the sunlight required by other plants and marine animals.[68]

The most serious long-term consequence of automotive emissions, however, is the atmospheric buildup of CO_2 and other "greenhouse"

"Between 1976 and 1986,
the average lead level
in Americans' blood
dropped more than a third."

gases—nitrous oxide, methane, and ozone. There is now virtual consensus among scientists that if the concentration of CO_2 in the atmosphere doubles, a substantial increase in global temperature will occur. Indeed, recent research indicates that a rise in temperature is already under way. The impending climate change could shift global precipitation patterns, disrupt crop growing regions, raise sea levels, and threaten coastal cities worldwide with inundation.[69]

Among all the auto-generated air pollutants, lead has been most successfully fought. Since it was purposely added to gasoline as an octane enhancer, it could just as well be eliminated from it. Lead's adverse health effects were recognized almost as soon as it was introduced in the early twenties. Fifty years later, the toll on human health could no longer be denied: Lead is known to cause neurological disorders, brain damage, and learning disabilities; it can damage the kidney, liver, reproductive system, and blood formation and can complicate pregnancies. Lead is now suspected to have significant effects at much lower concentrations in the bloodstream than formerly considered "safe." By strange coincidence, it turned out that catalytic converters—the equipment introduced in the mid-seventies to reduce emissions of hydrocarbons and carbon monoxide—can only function properly on lead-free gasoline. Thus, health and technical reasons made banning lead imperative.[70]

The United States and Japan have led the effort to reduce the use of lead, and a large fraction of their car fleets can now run on unleaded gas. Between 1976 and 1986, total annual lead emissions in the United States decreased by 94 percent. The health benefits are unequivocal: Over the same period, the average lead level in Americans' blood dropped more than a third.[71]

Australia, Brazil, Canada, and New Zealand are essentially proceeding along the same track as the United States. Eastern Europe is only beginning to introduce unleaded fuel, but because the volume of fuel consumption is comparatively small and governments control the production and distribution of cars and fuel, a swift changeover may well be possible.[72]

In Western Europe, on the other hand, progress in eliminating lead has been comparatively slow and uneven. Commitments to phasing out lead—making unleaded gasoline widely available and pricing it attractively—are strongest in Austria, the Netherlands, Scandinavia, Switzerland, and West Germany. But elsewhere on the continent, motorists have very little access to unleaded supplies and no incentives to switch, even though EEC policy requires all members to make lead-free gasoline widely available by 1989 and to ensure that all new vehicles are capable of running on unleaded fuel. Overall, up to one-quarter of European cars may currently be able to run on unleaded fuel. As of 1986, however, unleaded gasoline had a market share of no more than 5 percent. The Commission of the European Communities estimates that lead-free gasoline will account for 83 percent of sales by 2000.[73]

No such easy remedies are available for the other automotive pollutants. Fuel efficiency can help reduce emissions by virtue of burning less fuel. Reducing the weight of a vehicle and/or the size of the engine cuts down on CO_2, particulate matter, and nitrogen oxides. But catalytic converters are far more effective for reducing hydrocarbon and carbon monoxide emissions. Fuel injection reduces carbon monoxide, nitrogen oxides, and volatile organic compound evaporative emissions as well as fuel consumption. One technology under development is a membrane that, by separating nitrogen from the air before it is drawn into the combustion chamber, would not only eliminate nitrogen oxides but also boost combustion efficiency.[74]

Pollution abatement is complicated by the fact that controlling one or more pollutants may in some cases be achieved only at the expense of increases in others. For example, lean-burn engines (with an air-to-fuel ratio of 20 to 1 or more instead of the conventional 15 to 1) allow more-efficient fuel combustion and reduce the emission of nitrogen oxides and carbon monoxide, but tend to increase hydrocarbon discharges. And while a catalytic converter reduces carbon monoxide, it slightly increases CO_2 and sulfur dioxide emissions. Furthermore, the control system chosen has an important impact on fuel economy. Initially, the technologies used in the early seventies to meet U.S.

"Fuel efficiency
can help reduce emissions
by virtue of burning
less fuel."

emission standards led to fuel economy penalties of up to 2 percent; more advanced control technologies introduced subsequently, however, have actually helped improve vehicle fuel economy.[75]

39

Automotive pollution control in the United States has passed through three stages. Initially, engine modifications involving exhaust gas recirculation, lower compression ratios, leaner air-to-fuel ratios, and electronic controls were applied. Beginning in 1975, oxidation catalysts were introduced that transform hydrocarbons and carbon monoxide into water vapor and CO_2. More sophisticated three-way catalysts, which in addition reduce emissions of nitrogen oxides, were introduced in 1980.[76]

Over the life of a vehicle, today's catalysts cut hydrocarbon emissions by an average of 87 percent, carbon monoxide by 85 percent, and nitrogen oxides by 62 percent. They are even more effective when they are new, reducing hydrocarbons by 93 percent, carbon monoxide by 98 percent, and nitrogen oxides by 76 percent. Although these devices have been improved over the years, they can never be completely effective. Inspection and maintenance programs are crucial. And catalysts are least effective when an engine is cold—a frequent situation given the prevalence of short trips in OECD member countries.[77]

Since the early sixties, the United States and Japan have set the pace in establishing emission limits and pioneering control devices. Permissible U.S. emissions were tightened from an uncontrolled level of 10 grams per mile for hydrocarbons in the sixties to 0.41 grams per mile now, from 80 to 3.4 grams per mile for carbon monoxide, and from 4 to 1 gram per mile for nitrogen oxides. Japan's standards, implemented in 1975 and 1978, are roughly comparable.[78]

Australia, Canada, and South Korea recently established emission standards equivalent to those in force in the United States. Brazil initiated a 10-year phase-in of regulations that, by 1997, will allow it to match current U.S. standards. Emissions in Argentina, India, and Mexico, on the other hand, still go virtually uncontrolled; Chilean emission control laws have actually been relaxed under the Pinochet regime. Emission controls in the Soviet Union and Eastern Europe are limited to engine modifications.[79]

Within Western Europe, there is a widening gulf between the so-called Stockholm group and the European Community. Austria, Norway, Sweden, and Switzerland require installation of catalytic converters and compliance with emission levels comparable to those prevalent in the United States. EEC emission standards, which establish separate categories for large, medium, and small vehicles, are considerably less stringent.

While the EEC requirements for large cars come relatively close to existing U.S. standards, those for small cars—some 60 percent of the autos on the road in Europe—are still very lenient. Because some 70 to 85 percent of all French, Spanish, and Italian cars are small, very little reduction in emissions can be expected in these countries. Even though Western Europe has fewer cars than the United States and the cars do not travel as far, they now emit as much or perhaps even slightly more pollutants than American cars do.[80]

Profound disagreements among EEC members over standards, speed of change, and enforcement stalled progress for years. The current standards are no more than the lowest common denominator. At the national level, Denmark has demanded tighter standards, and West Germany and the Netherlands provide tax incentives for car buyers purchasing less polluting vehicles.[81]

Europe has also been slow to control diesel pollutants, even though diesels are enjoying rising popularity, unlike in Japan and the United States. In 1986, they captured 18 percent of the new-car market. Low exhaust temperatures and the presence of solid particulate matter in the exhaust make the application of catalytic converters much more difficult on diesels. Efforts have instead been directed at electronic control systems, electrostatic traps, and ceramic exhaust filters. EEC diesel emissions standards are still much looser than those in the United States, which ironically many European-produced vehicles are already capable of meeting.[82]

The net result of this patchwork of standards in industrial countries is that emission controls have been most successful in reducing carbon monoxide and hydrocarbons. During the seventies, carbon monoxide emissions from mobile sources fell by more than 50 percent in Japan and by one-third in the United States. But during the eighties progress has come to a virtual standstill, even though emission levels remain unacceptably high. In most of Europe, carbon monoxide emissions are on the rise as traffic volume increases. Hydrocarbon emissions show a roughly similar trend. Emissions of nitrogen oxides stabilized or decreased modestly in the seventies and early eighties in the United States, Japan, and some European countries. But more recently, rising traffic volumes appear to have wiped out earlier gains. In the United States (and presumably elsewhere), particulates and sulfur dioxide discharges are still on the rise.[83]

Air quality in the United States has improved, but the goal of clean air remains elusive. Even though U.S. emission standards are as strict as any in the world, the nation's enormous traffic volume threatens to overwhelm pollution control efforts. The average daily ozone concentration in U.S. cities decreased by 15 percent from 1975 to 1981, but only half that much since then. Some 59 American cities still do not meet federal carbon monoxide standards, and a further 9 are also out of compliance with ozone standards. One-third of them have no prospect of ever meeting them. Los Angeles, by far the worst offender, violated federal ozone standards on 143 days during 1985–87.[84]

The federal government and many state and local authorities have failed to take bold action in combatting air pollution. Numerous cities have not developed or implemented adequate plans to meet federal air quality standards. The Clean Air Act calls for bans on federal funds for new highway and industrial construction in noncompliance areas, but the Environmental Protection Agency (EPA) has been lax in enforcement. Congress has repeatedly rolled back the deadline for meeting ozone standards—from 1975 to 1982, then to 1987, and now to August 1988. Senate and House bills to reauthorize the Clean Air Act would extend attainment deadlines by 3 to 15 years, but would tighten emission standards and impose stricter pollution control requirements.[85]

There is little hope that air quality can be improved with current measures. While U.S. standards are still serving as a roadmap for emission control in other countries, they are clearly not tight enough to chart the course toward clean air. The average new gasoline-powered car could already meet considerably more stringent norms than those in force today. Yet there are no in-use standards for older cars, even though these often pollute far more than permitted by new-car standards.[86]

Rising numbers of cars, higher speeds, the lack of further progress in fuel economy, and the popularity of light trucks (which are more polluting than passenger cars) all call for much tougher measures. EPA Administrator Lee Thomas has suggested that "the smog problem may well need to be dealt with by reducing the number of cars on the street, by telling people they can't drive nearly to the extent they have in the past." Indeed, Athens and Budapest have recently imposed strict restraints on motorized traffic in their inner cities in an effort to combat urban air pollution.[87]

Pollution abatement efforts everywhere have focused almost entirely on tailpipe devices that seek to reduce exhaust emissions rather than on developing solutions that might prevent their formation in the first place. As Barry Commoner, Director of the Center for Biology of Natural Systems in New York, points out, auto manufacturers and government regulators have given insufficient attention to the difficult but more productive task of changing the basic technologies—that is, the engine design—that produce the pollutants.[88]

Some of the alternative designs described earlier as fuel savers are also pollution abaters. The stratified-charge engine is capable of running on a multitude of fuels and can operate at high compression ratios without subjecting the air in the cylinder to excessive temperatures, thus sharply suppressing the formation of nitrogen oxides. The adiabatic diesel engine provides high fuel efficiency and could safely meet all U.S. emission standards except for nitrogen oxides, which may require exhaust gas recirculation. Ceramic engines or engine components applied to both spark-plug and diesel engines could also

"Manufacturers and regulators
have given insufficient attention
to the difficult but productive task
of changing basic technologies
that produce pollutants."

cut emissions. Unfortunately, government R&D support for these technologies in the United States has been terminated or sharply curtailed under the Reagan administration.[89]

The use of nonpetroleum fuels to reduce emissions is garnering growing support among both public officials and auto industry managers. Current efforts, particularly in the United States, focus primarily on the use of alcohol fuels. A bill passed by both houses of Congress eases corporate fuel economy standards for those companies that produce either "dedicated" alternative-fuel vehicles (designed to use a fuel mixture containing at least 85 percent ethanol or methanol) or fuel-flexible vehicles (capable of running on various blends of gasoline and alcohol fuels or of operating on natural gas and gasoline). The intent is to encourage automakers to mass-produce such cars.[90]

Owing to its high cost, ethanol is likely to be used in relatively small quantities, in alcohol blends (gasoline containing up to 10 percent ethanol or methanol). Methanol, on the other hand, is expected to play a bigger role. Several states, among them Arizona, Colorado, Illinois, Iowa, Minnesota, and New Mexico, are considering mandating alcohol blends to reduce carbon monoxide levels and to meet Clean Air Act standards. About one-third of all motor fuels sold in Iowa are now blended with grain alcohol. Colorado hopes to reduce carbon monoxide levels by 14 percent during the winter and possibly by 25 percent in big cities through the use of these "oxygenated" fuels.[91]

California has taken the lead on pure methanol. The mecca of the automotive culture originally embraced methanol in 1979 in response to the oil crisis; the program has since gained fresh impetus as a way to meet air quality standards. A demonstration project currently involves 500-600 cars and buses. In little more than a decade, California hopes to replace as much as 30 percent of gasoline consumption with methanol in areas violating federal air pollution standards. The methanol is to be derived from natural gas in the near term and from coal in the long term.[92]

Both methanol and alcohol blends promise air quality benefits but also have drawbacks. Pure methanol yields only negligible amounts of highly reactive, ozone-producing hydrocarbons, but does not noticeably reduce carbon monoxide emissions; methanol blends decrease carbon monoxide emissions, but do not provide any tangible benefit on ozone. Cars burning pure methanol also emit two to five times as much formaldehyde as gasoline vehicles do. Formaldehyde not only may cause cancer, but also is a very active component in the ozone formation process. Tests for methanol vehicles show a wide range of air quality results, and there is considerable controversy over the merits of methanol use. Its environmental benefits appear the least ambiguous when used in diesel engines, where it would halve emissions of nitrogen oxides and virtually eliminate those of particulates, sulfur, and polycyclic aromatic hydrocarbons.[93]

One aspect of turning to methanol that is frequently overlooked is the impact on the "greenhouse" effect. Methanol vehicles emit less CO_2 than gasoline-powered cars do. But producing the fuel from coal would worsen the threat of climate change because converting coal into methanol could double CO_2-equivalent emissions. Using natural gas instead as a feedstock would reduce these emissions only slightly compared with gasoline-fueled cars.[94]

The search for less polluting alternatives to petroleum extends beyond alcohol fuels. Outside the United States, natural gas vehicles are receiving growing attention. They lend themselves particularly well to high-compression lean-burn technology. Their greater combustion efficiency gives them an estimated 6-15 percent fuel efficiency advantage over conventional gasoline models and lower carbon monoxide and particulate emissions, but perhaps higher emissions of nitrogen oxides. These cars would reduce CO_2-equivalent emissions only moderately, because lower CO_2 emissions are partly offset by higher discharges of methane, a potent greenhouse gas.[95]

Electric vehicles essentially emit no pollutants. Their environmental acceptability, however, depends on how the electricity that powers them is generated. Nonfossil feedstocks would be most ideal. Using electricity derived from the current mix of power sources in the

> "Substantial benefits in
> reducing air pollution and averting
> a further buildup of greenhouse gases
> would be derived from a shift
> to hydrogen."

United States, an electric vehicle would release about the same amount of CO_2 as a gasoline-fueled car, more sulfur dioxide, but much lower amounts of other pollutants. Electric cars running on coal-produced electricity would substantially increase the amount of CO_2 released.[96]

45

Hydrogen may be the most desirable fuel of the future. It burns most efficiently in lean fuel mixtures, and is 15-45 percent more energy-efficient than gasoline. Unless the source is fossil fuels, the production of hydrogen does not lead to CO_2 emissions. Its use does not generate carbon monoxide or unburnt hydrocarbons, and emissions of nitrogen oxides are low. Similarly, if electricity derived from photovoltaics, wind, hydropower, or geothermal power is used, the generation of hydrogen through electrolysis does not entail any environmental cost.[97]

Pollution control measures to date—in the few countries where they have been implemented—have helped improve air quality. Yet ongoing mass motorization is threatening to wipe out the gains made so far. And government policymakers and corporate managers have yet to address the threat of climate change. The laws of thermodynamics effectively prevent the development of any devices to control CO_2 emissions because more energy would have to be expended to capture the carbon dioxide than is actually derived from the fuel to drive an automobile. Most immediately, improved fuel efficiency can help to reduce carbon dioxide emissions. But in the longer run, the world needs to adopt fuels that produce neither CO_2 nor any of the other pollutants in large quantities.[98]

Support for methanol has become fashionable because its large-scale use promises significant fringe benefits for the coal industry and the farm sector. But methanol fails the most crucial litmus test: It is unlikely to be produced from renewable sources in significant amounts and its environmental benefits are ambiguous. The most substantial benefits in reducing air pollution and averting a further buildup of greenhouse gases would be derived from a shift to hydrogen or electricity derived from renewable resources.

Reshaping Transportation

46 The auto culture is so deeply ingrained in western society that alternatives to it seem virtually unthinkable. But excessive reliance on cars can actually stifle rather than advance societies. The very success of mass motorization has created conditions that cannot be ameliorated simply by making cars more efficient and less polluting.

The automobile exacts an enormous toll in human life. Despite safety improvements, more than 200,000 people died in traffic accidents around the world in 1985, with millions more suffering injuries of varying severity. In several developing countries, where fatalities per mile traveled are often 20 times higher than in industrial ones, traffic accidents are now a leading cause of death.[99]

Large stretches of land have been given over to the automobile and its infrastructure. Parking a car at home, the office, and the shopping mall requires on average 4,000 square feet of asphalt. Over 60,000 square miles of land in the United States have been paved over: That works out to about 2 percent of the total surface area, and to 10 percent of all arable land. Worldwide, at least a third of an average city's land is devoted to roads, parking lots, and other elements of a car infrastructure. In American cities, close to half of all the urban space goes to accommodate the automobile; in Los Angeles, the figure reaches two-thirds.[100]

Cars confer on their owners virtually limitless freedom as long as their numbers remain limited. But instead of facilitating individual mobility, the proliferation of automobiles has bred a crisis of its own—congestion. This is as much the case in industrial nations, where cars are incredibly numerous, as in developing countries, where fewer vehicles crowd still fewer roads and compete for space with buses, rickshaws, bicycles, animal-drawn carts, and pedestrians. Those cities most reliant on automobiles face virtual paralysis, an "urban thrombosis," as Kirkpatrick Sale has put it, "that slowly deprives the city of its lifeblood."[101]

Average car travel speeds are reportedly as low as 8 miles per hour (MPH) in London, and even less in Tokyo. The conventional approach to the congestion problem has led to a vicious circle: Building more roads simply attracts more cars, thus increasing the pressure for still more roads. In southern California, where there are probably more miles of freeways than anywhere else in the world and where daily commutes of 40 miles are not uncommon, the average travel speed is no higher than 33 MPH. It is expected to drop to 15 MPH by 2000, as population and car ownership continue to grow rapidly. The Commission on California State Government Organization and Economy, a panel of business and political leaders, recently warned that mounting congestion had placed California on the brink of "a transportation crisis which will affect the economic prosperity of the state."[102]

47

Congestion is more than an annoyance. The U.S. Department of Transportation estimated that due to congestion, nearly 3 billion gallons of gasoline were wasted in the United States in 1984, accounting for roughly 4 percent of the nation's annual gasoline consumption. The Department projects that over 7 billion gallons of fuel will be wasted by 2005 on highways alone, assuming no additional road construction.[103]

Most North American and Australian cities bear the imprint of the automobile system. In effect, they have become "segmented" communities. Residential settlements are dispersed in sprawling suburbs, far from city centers where jobs used to be concentrated. Employment has followed the same track: Two-thirds of all jobs created in the United States from 1960 to 1980 were located in the suburbs, and the trend has further accelerated in the current decade. As a result, the number of commutes within central city areas has remained fairly stable, while the number of trips between central cities and suburbs and from suburb to suburb has doubled within the same period of time. When suburban communities are too scattered to be served efficiently, public mass transit is not feasible. Similarly, walking and biking are not serious options, because distances are mostly too great and sidewalks and bicycle lanes are relatively rare. The automobile actually has created more distance than it overcomes.[104]

In U.S. cities like Denver, Houston, and Los Angeles, roughly 90 percent of people get to work by car; in the less auto-dependent cities like New York, cars still account for two-thirds of all work-related trips. By comparison, in Europe, where communities are less extensively suburbanized and average commuting distances are half those of North America, only about 40 percent of urban residents use their cars. Some 37 percent use public transportation and the remainder walk or bike. In Tokyo, just 15 percent of the population drives to work.[105]

Americans retain the highest degree of individual mobility in the world. But their heavy reliance on the automobile is a peculiar blend of preference and necessity, a cross between an abiding love affair with the passenger car and a profound lack of alternatives to it. Fewer than 20 percent of the miles traveled by Americans in their cars are for vacationing, "pleasure" driving, or visiting family or friends. The overwhelming majority of driving goes for such daily necessities as commuting to work and shopping.[106]

A full accounting of the manifold subsidies the automobile receives, plus the environmental and health costs it entails, might cool the passion felt for cars. In most if not all countries, car owners do not bear the full costs of road building and maintenance, municipal services (such as traffic regulation and costs borne by police and fire departments), accidents and related health care, and tax losses from land paved over for automotive purposes.

In the United States, total subsidies may surpass $300 billion each year—an amount equal to all personal auto-related expenditures. A preliminary, conservative estimate puts the subsidy at some $2,400 for every passenger car. If these expenses were reflected in retail fuel prices, a gallon of gasoline might cost as much as $4.50. Furthermore, other, less quantifiable environmental costs of the auto system are disregarded in conventional analyses as mere "externalities." An environment tax, assessed either on automobiles or fuels, would help internalize these costs. No doubt political opposition to such measures would be enormous. But societies cannot continue to ignore the true costs of the automobile system.[107]

"Americans'
heavy reliance on the automobile
is a cross between an abiding
love affair with the passenger car
and a profound lack of alternatives."

With a short reprieve from higher oil prices, it is time to build a bridge from an auto-centered society into an alternative transportation future characterized by greater diversity of transport modes, in which cars, buses, rail systems, bicycles, and walking all complement each other. Michael Replogle of the Institute for Transportation and Development Policy in Washington, D.C., notes that "just as an ecological system is healthiest when it displays great diversity and differentiation, so too is a transportation system most healthy and robust when diverse modal options are available to those moving people or goods. A transportation system dependent on only one or two modes of transport is far more susceptible to disruption and system failure."[108]

A first step that governments can take to minimize that susceptibility is to discourage auto use where possible. Local and national governments already impose a variety of physical and financial constraints on automobile use in particular areas or at specific times. Special lanes for high-occupancy vehicles, for example, promote ride-sharing. Area licensing schemes, access fees to congested roads, fees for low-occupancy vehicles, and parking controls are being tested around the world with varying degrees of commitment and success.[109]

Public transportation systems offer a host of advantages over automobiles. When fully used, they are considerably more energy-efficient and generally less polluting. In addition, public mass transit reduces congestion: A car requires roughly nine times more road space per passenger than a bus. Running on tracks or lanes separate from cars, rail systems and buses can provide rapid transit.[110]

Despite high levels of car ownership, Western Europe has always boasted an extensive and reliable network of public mass transit systems—buses, streetcars, subways, and railroads. In the United States, by contrast, public transportation plays a marginal role. It is almost forgotten today that there used to be a network of efficient and well-functioning urban and interurban rail systems—so-called trolleys. By 1917, there were nearly 45,000 miles of trolley tracks. Together with bus systems, they attracted more than 20 billion passengers yearly in the twenties and then, for a short time during World War II, more than 25 billion.[111]

50

Beginning in the thirties, General Motors—together with counterparts in the oil, steel, and tire industries—acquired more than 100 electric rail systems in 45 cities, dismantled the electric lines, and paved over the tracks. By the late fifties, about 90 percent of the trolley network had been eliminated.[112]

After the first oil crisis, U.S. public mass transit reversed the steady decline in ridership that had taken place ever since the mid-forties. Today, there is a modest renaissance of the trolley in the United States. New systems have been built during the eighties in Buffalo, Portland, Sacramento, and San Diego. After realizing that excessive reliance on private passenger cars could threaten their economic vitality, such auto-dependent cities as Dallas, Houston, and Los Angeles are planning or in the process of constructing such systems. At the same time, surviving systems in San Francisco, Boston, and Pittsburgh are being upgraded and extended.[113]

Each particular urban or suburban setting determines which mode of public transport is most adequate. A subway system may be preferable where the right-of-way above ground is not available or where urban densities make ground transportation impractical. Subways usually have the greatest capacity to transport large numbers of passengers at high speed. But "light rail" systems are considerably cheaper to construct than underground metros. Buses are by far the cheapest mode of public transportation, but they pollute more and, unless separate express lanes are established, they get caught up in road congestion. In interurban and rural transportation, European rail systems have demonstrated efficiency, speed, and convenience that rival the automobile.[114]

Public transportation is relatively limited in the routes it serves, how many stops it makes, and how frequently it runs. But if properly planned, public transit networks can approximate the flexibility provided by private passenger cars. Single-destinational systems essentially serve the "downtown" area of a city, but provide little access to elsewhere; transfer possibilities are limited to the central business district. Multidestinational or grid systems, on the other hand, allow convenient transfers between different bus and rail lines by syn-

"Reorienting transportation priorities
can be successful
only within the framework of
a comprehensive urban policy."

chronizing schedules. They enhance access throughout a metro-
politan area and create a dense network of mass transit corridors that
attracts more riders. Multidestinational systems are operating successfully in many European and some North American cities.[115]

The viability of public transit systems—particularly in suburban
areas—can be enhanced by making them more accessible. Bike-and-
ride stations and facilities to carry bicycles on buses and rail systems
have proved enormously popular in Denmark, Japan, the
Netherlands, and West Germany. In the United States, by contrast,
transit access by bicycle remains underutilized even though it has
grown substantially since the early seventies. Instead, automobile
access (park-and-ride lots) has been given priority by transportation
planners.[116]

An extensive bike-and-ride system could provide significant benefits.
The average American automobile commuter can reduce his or her
annual use of gasoline by some 407 gallons—equivalent to half the
gasoline burned up by a typical car in the United States in a year—by
switching to bike-and-ride. A 1980 Chicago Area Transportation
Study found that improving bicycle access to public transit is the
most cost-effective way to reduce auto emissions. Thus, transit servic-
ability standards need to be adopted that allow easy access to public
transit.[117]

Reorienting transport priorities can be successful only within the
framework of a comprehensive urban policy. There is a symbiotic
relationship between land use patterns and transportation networks.
Public transit systems can facilitate and reinforce more compact land
use, while land use patterns frequently determine transportation
needs. For example, car dependency can be decreased by zoning
ordinances that encourage a higher density of urban activity while
slowing development at the urban perimeter. The more concentrated
both population and jobs are, the shorter are travel distances, the
more mass transit becomes viable, and the more walking and biking
occurs. In short, more compact cities foster less individual motorized
transport.[118]

To encourage people to live close to where their jobs are, housing needs to be affordable. Designing urban areas to favor walking and biking not only reduces car dependency but also provides the additional benefit of maintaining vital and attractive cities. Under the Dutch *woonerf* concept, for instance, residential streets are not exclusively reserved for motorized transport but are transformed into public spaces. Many other European inner-city areas enjoyed a strong revival in the seventies with the establishment of extensive pedestrian zones.[119]

Suburbanization cannot simply be reversed. But suburbs are most vulnerable to any future oil shortages or restraints on auto use that may be taken to curb pollution. If these communities are to enhance their future viability, they need to become more self-contained—that is, to evolve into subcenters that may be less urban in character than traditional cities, but more compact than they currently are. In the United States, even though suburbanization continues at an unhealthy pace, some town designers and developers are rejecting the dominant suburban-style residential areas in favor of a "neo-traditionalist" approach of creating more urbane, walkable communities that encourage sociability and a less frantic way of living.[120]

Third World cities stand at a crossroads as they swell in size and as urban transportation needs rapidly multiply. In the view of Michael Replogle, "there is a growing transportation crisis in many lesser developed countries. This crisis is the product of . . . a mismatch between the supply of transportation infrastructure, services, and technologies and the mobility needs of the majority of Third World people."[121]

Alas, government policies favoring private car ownership by a tiny but affluent elite are squandering scarce resources and distorting development priorities. Importing fuels, car components, or already assembled autos stretches import budgets thin. In Haiti, for example, only 1 out of every 200 people owns a car, yet fully one-third of the country's import budget is devoted to fuel and transport equipment.[122]

Likewise, building and maintaining an elaborate system of roads, highways, bridges, and tunnels devours enormous resources. The sixties and seventies saw a road-building boom in many developing nations, to the detriment of railways and other forms of transport. With insufficient resources for maintenance, a substantial backlog of roads are in disrepair: One-quarter to one-third of all Third World roads are in poor condition, with another 40 percent deemed to be in only fair condition.[123]

Existing public transportation—most commonly bus systems—often is in poor repair and has failed to keep up with urban population growth. In India and Bangladesh, for example, the urban public transit sector may meet as little as 15 percent of transportation needs. Yet the urban poor spend a disproportionate share of their incomes on transport. In New Delhi, the lowest income groups devote 20-25 percent of their household incomes to transport, while the wealthiest group spends only 8 percent. And often the poor cannot afford public transportation at all. Walking accounts for two-thirds of all trips in large African cities like Kinshasa, and for almost half the trips in Bangalore, India.[124]

Governments and international agencies frequently assign priority to motorized travel in traffic planning, budget decisions, and allocation of street space. Pedestrians and traditional modes of transportation are increasingly being marginalized. Third World cities such as Jakarta and Manila have imposed constraints on nonmotorized forms of travel; others, such as Singapore and Caracas, provide insufficient sidewalk space.[125]

Unfortunately, the World Bank has helped to slant transportation projects toward motorized solutions. Between 1972 and 1985, rail and bus systems received less than one-third of the funding for World Bank urban transportation projects. Nonmotorized modes have been virtually ignored. The car culture is so pervasive that the search for what has been billed as "appropriate car technology"—for example, the effort to introduce a sturdy, relatively low-cost Africar—has taken precedence over serious reflections about affordable and sustainable transportation.[126]

To meet the mobility needs of the poor majority in the Third World, substantial improvements and expansion of public transport are required. Subway systems once were regarded as ideal solutions for burgeoning Third World cities because of their ability to move large numbers of passengers at high speed. But the heavy initial investment is beyond the financial capabilities of most urban governments. Fares have to be high to cover capital and operating costs—too high to attract enough riders—or subsidies need to be astronomically high. Calcutta and Cairo recently completed such subway systems, but many other municipalities have been forced to postpone construction of planned systems indefinitely. Cheaper light rail systems are now a more favored option.[127]

Nonmotorized modes of transportation that require little input of capital and energy can be an important complement to public transit. Such low-cost, informal modes could also generate a significant amount of employment. They are more affordable, mostly do not pollute, and do not strain investment and import budgets. In Asia, for example, human-powered rickshaws, pedicabs (motorcycle-driven rickshaws), bicycles, push-carts, and tongas (animal-drawn carts) fill the gap left by inadequate public transportation. Engineering improvements can make them more efficient.[128]

Bicycles—considered mainly a recreational device in the industrial West —are the predominant means of short-distance urban vehicular transportation in Asia, although they are far less common in parts of the western hemisphere and Africa. An average bicycle requires only 2 percent of the capital necessary to own and operate a car. India has approximately 25 times as many bicycles as motor vehicles. In China, rising per capita incomes have triggered a bicycle boom; there is now one bicycle for every four people, and in cities, one for every two. This impressive increase in bicycles has not yet received as much attention as the much smaller rise in car ownership.[129]

A key measure for the Third World is the provision of cheap credit for the purchase of low-cost vehicles. In Hyderabad, India, commercial banks have been encouraged to lend money to rickshaw operators at preferential rates. If such vehicles are produced locally, they do not

"The proliferation of automobiles
has led to the multiple crises
of oil depletion, air pollution,
looming climate change, and congestion."

strain a country's import budget, while at the same time providing employment opportunities. Mexico and China, for example, have fostered domestic bicycle industries. Such policies are essential if countries are to move beyond exclusive reliance on the automobile and toward more practical alternatives.[130]

French philosopher André Gorz once remarked that "the automobile is the paradoxical example of a luxury object that has been devalued by its own spread. But this practical devaluation has not yet been followed by an ideological devaluation." The proliferation of automobiles has led to the multiple crises of oil depletion, air pollution, looming climate change, and congestion. The magnitude of these problems suggests the need for a fundamental rethinking of the automobile's role.[131]

The scope of the modern, auto-centered transportation system, from production and distribution to operation and repair, is so tremendous that fundamental change cannot occur quickly. Those who depend on automobiles for their livelihoods—the oil and auto industries, highway lobby groups, and government transport planning departments—form a powerful constituency. Decision-making structures hence strongly favor the status quo. A successful policy therefore must have various layers, ranging from measures that can take effect immediately to others that will need more time to make their impact felt.

Making cars more efficient and less polluting remains an imperative first goal in both developing and industrial countries, along with steps to discourage auto use where possible. Considerably more vigorous efforts are needed to identify and develop an alternative to petroleum-based fuels that is both renewable and environmentally acceptable. Hydrogen scores well in these regards but fares badly on the priority list of governments and private corporations. A considerably more extensive research and development program is needed if hydrogen is to become a viable option.

Transport and land use change slowly, but shape our societies in a profound manner. Planning in these vital areas has to become far better integrated and coordinated to reduce the need for individual motorized transportation. As part of the bridge into a more balanced transportation future, the automobile's numerous subsidies and hidden costs must be taken into account. Far greater resources need to be devoted to building or expanding efficient and flexible public mass transit systems.

A more comprehensive transportation policy must recognize that transportation needs are not abstract. What people need is access to jobs, homes, and services. More compact and integrated communities can provide such access without long commutes. If urban design—creating new communities as well as reshaping existing urban landscapes—can become an integral component of future transportation policies, the contrasting individual interests in mobility and societal interests in fuel supply security, environmental protection, and urban integrity may be reconciled.

Notes

1. Production figures based on Motor Vehicle Manufacturers Association (MVMA), *Facts and Figures '88* (Detroit, Mich.: 1988).

2. "The Unfinished Revolution" (editorial), *The Economist*, January 25, 1986.

3. Ibid.

4. Production and ownership data from MVMA, *World Motor Vehicle Data, 1987 Edition* (Detroit, Mich.: 1987) and MVMA, *Facts and Figures '87* (Detroit, Mich.: 1987).

5. MVMA, *World Motor Vehicle Data, 1988 Edition* (Detroit, Mich.: 1988).

6. Ibid.

7. Ibid.

8. Ibid.

9. Philip Patterson, "Periodic Energy Report, No. 2/1987," Department of Energy (DOE), Washington, D.C., December 1987.

10. Population data from United Nations, *World Population Prospects: Estimates and Projections as Assessed in 1984* (New York: 1986).

11. Toli Welihozkiy, "Automobiles and the Soviet Consumer," in *Soviet Economy in a Time of Change*, Vol. 1, Compendium of Papers Submitted to the U.S. Congress, Joint Economic Committee, October 10, 1979; "Russian Cars: French Accent," *The Economist*, December 3, 1983; MVMA, *World Motor Vehicle Data* (Detroit, Mich.: various editions).

12. Auto growth rates are based on MVMA, *Facts and Figures* (various editions).

13. Per capita income figures from Ruth Leger Sivard, *World Military and Social Expenditures 1987-88* (Washington, D.C.: World Priorities, 1988).

14. United Nations, *World Population Prospects*; MVMA, *Facts and Figures '87*.

15. "A Great Drive Forward," *Asiaweek*, December 11, 1987; "How China Boosts Her Car Industry," *China Daily*, July 3, 1987; "China Plans to Build More Cars," *China Daily*, June 25, 1987; "China's Carmakers: Far to Go," *The Economist*, December 14, 1985; P.T. Bangsberg, "Chinese Promoting New Auto Joint Venture," *Journal of Commerce*, November 30, 1987; John Elliott, "A 1950s Comeback," *Financial Times Motor Industry Survey*, October 14, 1986.

16. MVMA, *Facts and Figures '87*; Jackson Diehl, "Automotive Age—Brazil: Aiming for the World Market," *Washington Post*, July 12, 1983.

17. Pedro-Pablo Kuczynski, "The Outlook for Latin American Debt," *Foreign Affairs*, Fall 1987; William A. Orme, "End of Mexico's Oil Boom Era Has Meant Hardships for Citizens," *Washington Post*, August 16, 1987.

18. MVMA, *World Motor Vehicle Data, 1987*; James Bruce, "Autolatina Braces For Further Clash," *Journal of Commerce*, October 15, 1987; Richard J. Meislin, "Mexico Set to Revamp Troubled Auto Industry," *New York Times*, September 15, 1983.

19. Roger Cohen, "Brazil's Violent Economic-Policy Shifts Are Causing Havoc Among Auto Makers," *Wall Street Journal*, August 28, 1987; "The Giants Ship Out to Shape Up," *Gazeta Mercantil*, July 13, 1987; Amal Nag and Steve Frazier, "Despite Ford Venture, Mexico Faces Uphill Struggle to be Competitive," *Wall Street Journal*, January 11, 1984; David Gardner, "Aiming for Exports," *Financial Times Motor Industry Survey*, October 14, 1986.

20. "South-East Asian Cars: In the Pits," *The Economist*, August 13, 1983; P.T. Bangsberg, "Malaysia Plans to Sell Autos in U.S.," *Journal of Commerce*, February 8, 1988; "Proton Saga: Add a Little Matter," *The Economist*, August 1, 1987; Mark Wilson, "Thai Autos Delivered to Canada," *Journal of Commerce*, February 5, 1988; Clyde Farnsworth, "Administration Assails Soviet Car-Export Plan," *New York Times*, November 2, 1987; John Holusha, "The Disappearing 'U.S. Car'," *New York Times*, August 10, 1985. Counting in cars produced by foreign-owned plants in the United States, "imports" could reach a 50-percent market share within a few years; "Downsizing Detroit: The Big Three's Strategy for Survival," *Business Week*, April 14, 1986.

21. Alan Altshuler et al., *The Future of the Automobile: The Report of MIT's International Auto Program* (Cambridge, Mass.: MIT Press, 1984); export share based on MVMA, *World Motor Vehicle Data, 1987* and *Facts and Figures '87*.

22. Car density from MVMA, *Facts and Figures '87*; "Koreans Warned of Labor Violence; Car Exports Off Sharply," *New York Times*, September 6, 1987; Mark Clifford, "Labour Strikes Out," *Far Eastern Economic Review*, August 27, 1987.

23. DOE, *Assessment of Costs and Benefits of Flexible and Alternative Fuel Use in the U.S. Transportation Sector—Progress Report One: Context and Analytical Framework* (Washington, D.C.: 1988); transport sector consumption based on Patterson, "Periodic Energy Report," and on Mary C. Holcomb et al., *Transportation Energy Data Book: Edition 9* (Oak Ridge, Tenn.: Oak Ridge National Laboratory, 1987). Comparative international data for passenger cars only are not available.

24. Peter Newman and Jeffrey Kenworthy, "Gasoline Consumption and Cities—A Comparison of U.S. Cities With a Global Survey and Some Implications," Transport Research Paper 8/87, School of Environmental and Life Sciences, Murdoch University, Australia; Peter Newman and Jeffrey Kenworthy, "Transport and Urban Form in Thirty-Two of the World's Principal Cities," Paper for International Symposium on Transport, Communication and Urban Form, Monash University, August 24-26, 1987.

25. José Goldemberg et al., *Energy for Development* (Washington, D.C.: World Resources Institute, 1987).

26. On Brazilian oil import bills, see "Brazil Survey," *The Economist*, April 25, 1987; International Monetary Fund, *International Financial Statistics, 1987 Yearbook* (Washington, D.C.: 1987). A barrel of alcohol fuel costs about $45 to provide (compared with oil prices of $15-20), but its retail price is kept to no more than 65 percent of gasoline prices. Moreover, a reduced fuel import bill is at least partially offset by the need to import some $3 billion worth of foodstuffs that farmers stopped planting in order to grow sugarcane as an ethanol feedstock; Mark Kosmo, *Money to Burn? The High Costs of Energy Subsidies* (Washington, D.C.: World Resources Institute, 1987).

27. United Nations, *1985 Energy Statistics Yearbook* (New York: 1987).

28. James Tanner, "OPEC in a Few Years is Likely to Reassert Control Over Oil Markets," *Wall Street Journal*, August 21, 1987; British Petroleum Company (BP), *BP Statistical Review of World Energy* (London: 1987).

29. Production and import estimates based on DOE, Energy Information Administration (EIA), *Monthly Energy Review*, November 1987. U.S. imports are projected to surpass the 50-percent mark in the nineties; see DOE, *Energy Security* (Washington, D.C.: 1987).

30. BP, *Statistical Review*; Charles Ebinger, "Market Stability: Worth Paying the Price," *OPEC Bulletin*, September 1985.

31. Howard S. Geller, "Ethanol from Sugar Cane in Brazil," in Annual Reviews, Inc., *Annual Review of Energy, Vol. 10* (Palo Alto, Calif.: 1985); Cynthia Pollock Shea, *Renewable Energy: Today's Contribution, Tomorrow's Promise*, Worldwatch Paper 81 (Washington, D.C.: Worldwatch Institute, January 1988).

32. "PMAA Makes a Case for Methanol," *Energy Daily*, July 30, 1987; "Danish Farmers Mull Ethanol Unit," *European Energy Report*, September 4, 1987.

33. J.R. Kenworthy and P.W.G. Newman, "The Potential of Ethanol as a Transportation Fuel: A Review Based on Technological, Economic, and Environmental Criteria," Discussion Paper No. 6/86, Murdoch University, Aus-

tralia, August 1986; "Energy: Another Deficit," *The Economist*, November 14, 1987.

34. DOE, *Costs and Benefits of Flexible and Alternative Fuel Use*; Mark A. De-Luchi et al., "A Comparative Analysis of Future Transportation Fuels," Institute of Transportation Studies, University of California, Berkeley, October 1987; "Guzzling Gas," *Asiaweek*, August 9, 1987; "The Case for CNG and LPG as Auto Fuel Alternatives," *Daily Express* (Malaysia), August 20, 1987.

35. Peter Hoffmann, "Hydrogen: Power to Burn?" *Not Man Apart*, November/December 1987; "Hydrogen Drives Prototype Van," *New Scientist*, February 27, 1986.

36. DeLuchi et al., "Comparative Analysis of Future Transportation Fuels"; Paul J. Werbos, *Oil Dependency and the Potential for Fuel Cell Vehicles*, Technical Paper Series (Warrendale, Pa.: Society of Automotive Engineers (SAE), 1987).

37. DeLuchi et al., "Comparative Analysis of Future Transportation Fuels."

38. "Ethanol Dependent on Tax Subsidy, Study Says," *Energy Daily*, February 4, 1988; "EEC Says Ethanol Uneconomic," *European Energy Report*, August 7, 1987; on methanol, see California Council for Environmental and Economic Balance, *Alternative Fuels as an Air Quality Improvement Strategy—Prospects, Options, and Implications for California* (Sacramento, Calif.: November 1987); on natural gas, see DOE, *Costs and Benefits of Flexible and Alternative Fuel Use*; on hydrogen, see Peter Hoffmann, "Fueling the Future With Hydrogen," *Washington Post*, September 6, 1987.

39. Average fleet fuel economy from DOE, EIA, *Monthly Energy Review*, October 1987; new-car fuel economy from MVMA, *Facts and Figures '87*.

40. Fuel efficiency has been responsible for an estimated two-thirds of the reduced gasoline consumption per car in members of the Organisation for Economic Co-operation and Development (OECD), with the remainder due to reduced driving; International Energy Agency (IEA), *Energy Conservation in IEA Countries* and IEA, *Energy Policies and Programmes of IEA Countries, 1986 Review* (Paris: OECD, 1987).

41. Brazilian, Soviet, and East German fuel economy from William U. Chandler, *Energy Productivity: Key to Environmental Protection and Economic Progress*, Worldwatch Paper 63 (Washington, D.C.: Worldwatch Institute, January 1985).

42. MVMA, *Facts and Figures '87*; IEA, *Energy Conservation in IEA Countries*; R.M. Heavenrich et al., *Light Duty Automotive Trends Through 1986*, SAE Technical Paper Series (Warrendale, Pa.: SAE, 1986); Christopher Flavin and

Alan B. Durning, *Building on Success: The Age of Energy Efficiency*, Worldwatch Paper 82 (Washington, D.C.: Worldwatch Institute, March 1988).

43. On light trucks, see Philip Patterson, "Analysis of Future Transportation Petroleum Demand and Efficiency Improvements," presented at IEA Energy Demand Analysis Symposium, Paris, October 12-14, 1987; Patterson, "Periodic Energy Report." The trend toward larger cars in Europe is particularly strong in West Germany; Bundesministerium für Verkehr, *Verkehr in Zahlen 1987* (Bonn: September 1987).

44. Based on International Road Federation, *World Road Statistics* (Washington, D.C.: various issues).

45. Holcomb et al., *Transportation Energy Data Book*.

46. Worldwatch estimate.

47. Deborah Lynn Bleviss, *The New Oil Crisis and Fuel Economy Technologies: Preparing the Light Transportation Industry for the 1990's* (New York: Quorum Press, in press).

48. Ibid.; Philip Patterson, DOE, Washington, D.C., private communication, April 6, 1988; Heavenrich et al., *Light Duty Automotive Trends*.

49. Bleviss, *The New Oil Crisis*.

50. Julius J. Harwood, "Automakers Lighten the Load," *Technology Review*, July 1981; Holcomb et al., *Transportation Energy Data Book*.

51. Many plastics (the so-called thermosets) are not recyclable; thermoplastics, on the other hand, theoretically are recyclable, but high cost and the low quality of most residual products make waste separation and recovery unlikely; Klaus Müller, "The Increasing Use of Plastics and its Impacts on the Recyclability of Automobiles and on Waste Disposal in West Germany, the United States and Japan," presented at the Second Recycling Conference, Washington, D.C., June 18-19, 1987.

52. Bleviss, *The New Oil Crisis*.

53. Ibid.

54. OECD, *Environmental Effects of Automotive Transport* (The Compass Project) (Paris: 1986); Bleviss, *The New Oil Crisis*.

55. Bleviss, *The New Oil Crisis*; Patterson, private communication.

56. Bleviss, *The New Oil Crisis*.

57. Ibid. Vehicle acceleration also has a significant effect on fuel efficiency; Clarence Ditlow, Director, Center for Auto Safety, Washington, D.C., private communication, April 1, 1988.

58. Environmental Protection Agency (EPA), Inspection/Maintenance Staff, "Costs and Benefits of Tire Inflation in Inspection Programs," Ann Arbor, Mich., September 1981.

59. Bleviss, *The New Oil Crisis*; Dan McCosh, "Automotive Newsfront," *Popular Science*, December 1987.

60. Analyst quote is from Bleviss, *The New Oil Crisis*; Ford quote from Robert J. Golten et al. (eds.), *The End of the Road: A Citizen's Guide to Transportation Problemsolving* (Washington, D.C.: National Wildlife Federation/Environmental Action Foundation, Inc., 1977).

61. Worldwatch estimate, based on MVMA, *Facts and Figures '87*.

62. Joy Dunkerley and Irving Hoch, "The Pricing of Transport Fuels," *Energy Policy*, August 1986. Most developing countries subsidize diesel and kerosene, on which the urban poor rely most heavily; in Brazil, for example, diesel sells at a price 40 percent below that of gasoline. The implicit problem is that as the gap between these fuels grows too wide, cheaper diesel gets substituted for gasoline. Kosmo, *Money to Burn?*

63. The U.S. "gas guzzler" tax is assessed on the basis of a particular vehicle's fuel economy. However, it fails to encourage car buyers to purchase the most fuel-efficient models available: A 1986 car achieving a rating of more than 22.5 MPG was not subject to any levy, even while the government's own standards dictated a minimum corporate average fuel efficiency standard of 26 MPG. See Holcomb et al., *Transportation Energy Data Book*; Gary Klott, "Rise in 'Gas Guzzler' Tax Approved by Senate Panel," *New York Times*, March 22, 1988.

64. DeLuchi et al., "Comparative Analysis of Future Transportation Fuels"; "Auto Overuse = Dirty Air," *National Association of Railroad Passengers News*, February 1988.

65. Ariel Alexandre and Christian Avérous, "Transport's Toll on the Environment," *OECD Observer*, February/March 1988; CO_2 estimate from DeLuchi et al., "Comparative Analysis of Future Transportation Fuels." In the United States, highway transportation accounts for about 27 percent of all fossil-fuel-released CO_2.

66. Rose Marie Audette, "It Only Hurts When You Breathe," *Environmental Action*, March/April 1988; EPA, *The Economic Effects of Ozone on Agriculture* (Corvallis, Ore.: 1984). California's three principal crop harvests—cotton, grapes, and oranges—now suffer losses of up to 20 percent a year; Jay

Mathews, "Southern California Battling Smog With 'New Sense of Urgency'," *Washington Post*, March 14, 1988.

67. EPA, *National Air Quality and Emissions Trends Report, 1986* (Research Triangle Park, N.C.: 1988); "Central Budapest Car Ban Seeks to Curb Air Pollution," Reuters, March 30, 1988; Alan Cowell, "War on Smog is Rude Awakening for Athens," *New York Times*, February 14, 1988; Lester R. Brown and Jodi L. Jacobson, *The Future of Urbanization: Facing the Ecological and Economic Constraints*, Worldwatch Paper 77 (Washington, D.C.: Worldwatch Institute, May 1987).

68. Sandra Postel, *Air Pollution, Acid Rain, and the Future of Forests*, Worldwatch Paper 58 (Washington, D.C.: Worldwatch Institute, March 1984); Diane Fisher et al., "Polluted Coastal Waters: The Role of Acid Rain," Environmental Defense Fund, New York, April 1988.

69. Laura Tangley, "Preparing for Climate Change," *BioScience*, January 1988; Philip Shabecoff, "Temperature for World Rises Sharply in the 1980's," *New York Times*, March 29, 1988.

70. Barry Commoner, "A Reporter at Large: The Environment," *The New Yorker*, June 15, 1987; David Rosner and Gerald Markowitz, "Industry's 60-Year Fight Against Getting the Lead Out of the Air" (letter to the editor), *New York Times*, March 26, 1985; OECD, *Environmental Effects of Automotive Transport*.

71. EPA, *National Air Pollutant Emission Estimates, 1940-1985* (Research Triangle Park, N.C.: 1987); Michael Weisskopf, "EPA Backs Off Plans to Cut Lead Pollution of Air, Water," *Washington Post*, December 24, 1987. Even though roughly 90 percent of all gasoline-powered vehicles in the United States are legally required to use unleaded fuel, one-quarter of all gasoline sold is still leaded, which is cheaper than unleaded. OECD, *Environmental Effects of Automotive Transport*; Lee A. Daniels, "Debate Over New Fuel Lead Limit," *New York Times*, May 6, 1985; gas prices from DOE, *Monthly Energy Review*, October 1987. On lead level in blood, see Commoner, "A Reporter at Large."

72. SAE, *Motor Vehicle Pollution Control—A Global Perspective* (Warrendale, Pa.: 1987). East Germany now has a total of 22 unleaded pump-stations; *European Energy Report*, July 24, 1987.

73. "EC Lead-Free Fuel Plan is Moving Sluggishly," *International Herald Tribune*, July 10, 1987; "European Countries Proceeding Slowly to Comply With Unleaded Gas Directive," *World Environment Report*, June 11, 1987; "Lead Restrictions Make Slow Gains in Southern Europe," *World Environment Report*, September 3, 1987; OECD, *Environmental Effects of Automotive Transport*. On pricing policies, see "Lead-Free Incentives in Norway," *European Energy Report*, October 16, 1987; "Tax on West German Petrol," *European Energy Report*, October 2, 1987; "Unleaded Petrol: Heavy Going," *The Economist*, October 31, 1987; "French Lead-Free Moves Slowly," *European Energy Report*, July 24, 1987; E. Stanley Tucker, "Motor Vehicles: The Quest for Clean Air," *Petroleum Economist*, May 1986; "Unleaded Gasoline Going Slow in Penetration of European Markets," *Oil & Gas Journal*, January 25, 1988; Commission of the European Communities, *The State of the Environment in the European Community 1986* (Brussels: March 1987).

74. Jeff Alson, EPA, Emission Control Technology Division, Ann Arbor, Mich., private communications, February 24 and April 14, 1988. CO_2 emissions are inversely proportional to vehicle efficiency; thus, doubling fleet fuel economy will roughly halve CO_2 emissions. See DeLuchi et al., "Comparative Analysis of Future Transportation Fuels." The Japanese government has selected the nitrogen-separating membrane as one of the top technologies to be pursued in the next five years; in the United States, Dow Chemical is working on a similar membrane. Bleviss, *The New Oil Crisis*.

75. Lean-burn engines are still years away from meeting their emission and fuel economy targets. OECD, *Environmental Effects of Automotive Transport*; Michael P. Walsh, technical consultant on automotive emissions, private communications, March 15 and April 7, 1988; Alson, private communication; Bleviss, *The New Oil Crisis*.

76. OECD, *Energy and Cleaner Air* (Paris: 1987).

77. EPA, *Compilation of Air Pollutant Emission Factors—Volume II: Mobile Sources*, 4th ed. (Ann Arbor, Mich.: 1985); Alson, private communication; Walsh, private communication.

78. On U.S. standards, see Holcomb et al., *Transportation Energy Data Book*; OECD, *Energy and Cleaner Air*; Japanese standards from T. Karasudani, Japan External Trade Organization, New York, N.Y., private communication, February 24, 1988. Different driving cycles and types of instrumentation used make precise comparisons of national standards difficult.

79. Michael P. Walsh, "Worldwide Developments in Motor Vehicle Pollution Control—A 1987 Overview," and Alfred Szwarc and Gabriel Murgel Branco, "Automotive Emissions—The Brazilian Control Program," in SAE, *Motor Vehicle Pollution Control*; Sanjoy Hazarika, "New Delhi Struggles With Haze of Pollution," *New York Times*, January 10, 1988; Tyler Bridges, "Smog in Chilean Capital Rates With World's Worst," *Christian Science Monitor*, October 27, 1987.

80. Only the standards for large cars are stringent enough to warrant a three-way catalyst. Merrill Korth, EPA, Ann Arbor, Mich., private communication, February 24, 1988; H. Henssler and S. Gospage, "The Exhaust Emission

Standards of the European Community," in SAE, *Motor Vehicle Pollution Control*. The EEC is now considering tightening the standards for small cars; Walsh, private communication.

81. Walsh, private communication; Jane Leggett, "Reducing Motor Vehicle Pollution," *OECD Observer*, November 1986; Korth, private communication.

82. Walsh, "Worldwide Developments"; Alson, private communication.

83. Comparable data for air pollutants in OECD countries are sparse, and there is virtually no detailed information for the Third World. Only the United States, Canada, the United Kingdom, and, to a lesser degree, France, West Germany, and the Netherlands provide useful time series. See OECD, *OECD Environmental Data—Compendium 1987* (Paris: 1987); World Resources Institute/International Institute for Environment and Development, *World Resources 1987* (New York: Basic Books, 1987); Commission of the European Communities, *State of the Environment*; EPA, *Air Pollutant Estimates, 1940-1985*.

84. "EPA Chief Sees Auto Use Curbs," *Journal of Commerce*, March 9, 1988; Commoner, "A Reporter at Large"; EPA, *Air Pollutant Estimates, 1940-1985*. The failure to meet federal ozone standards is even more glaring in view of EPA's 1979 decision to raise the permissible ozone level in a one-hour period each year from 0.08 parts per million to 0.12. Recent studies indicate that several hours of exposure at lower levels may be dangerous to human health. See Mark D. Uehling, "Missing the Deadline on Ozone," *National Wildlife*, October/November 1987; Audette, "It Only Hurts When You Breathe"; Michael Weisskopf, "City Smog Worse in 1987, EPA Says," *Washington Post*, May 4, 1988.

85. Michael Weisskopf, "Hill Group Seeks to Clear the Air With Compromise on Smog Control," *Washington Post*, March 18, 1988; Audette, "It Only Hurts When You Breathe"; "EPA Punts on Construction Sanctions for City Ozone Violators," *Not Man Apart*, November/December 1987.

86. EPA, *Compilation of Emission Factors*; Alson, private communication. New amendments to the Clean Air Act now being discussed in the U.S. Congress would further reduce permissible emissions of hydrocarbons, nitrogen oxides, and particulates by half, but leave carbon monoxide standards unchanged. In effect, the bill would synchronize U.S. federal requirements with the stricter California standards. See "Clean Air Standards Attainment Act of 1987," Report of the Committee on Environment and Public Works, U.S. Senate, November 20, 1987.

87. Thomas quoted in "EPA Chief Sees Auto Use Curbs," *Journal of Commerce*; Cowell, "War on Smog"; "Central Budapest Car Ban," Reuters.

88. Commoner, "A Reporter at Large."

89. Carbon monoxide emissions of stratified-charge engines are lower, too, although hydrocarbon emissions may be somewhat higher than those of vehicles equipped with oxidation catalysts. OECD, *Environmental Effects of Automotive Transport*; Commoner, "A Reporter at Large." On ceramics, see Robert P. Larsen and Anant D. Vyas, "The Outlook for Ceramics in Heat Engines, 1990-2000: Results of a Worldwide Delphi Survey," Center for Transportation Research, Energy and Environmental Systems Division, Argonne National Laboratory, Argonne, Ill., March 1988. Other designs include the Stirling external combustion engine, the steam cycle engine, and the gas turbine engine; California Energy Commission, "Automotive and Fuel Technologies: Current and Future Options," Sacramento, Calif., March 1984.

90. U.S. Senate, Committee on Commerce, Science, and Transportation, "Report on Methanol and Alternative Fuels Promotion Act of 1987," U.S. Government Printing Office, Washington, D.C., 1987.

91. "Colorado Alternative Fuels Program to be Watched Carefully by Other States: Herman," *International Solar Energy Intelligence Report*, July 28, 1987; Warren Brown, "Alcohol May Make Comeback," *Washington Post*, June 28, 1987; "Only Methanol Looks Promising among Alternate Fuels, Oil Execs Say," *International Solar Energy Intelligence Report*, July 14, 1987.

92. "Air Quality Concerns Buoy Hopes for U.S. Makers of Alcohol Fuels," *Oil & Gas Journal*, February 9, 1987; Philip Shabecoff, "California Acts to Promote Switch From Gasoline to Methanol Fuel," *New York Times*, May 23, 1987. Officials claim that substituting methanol-fueled vehicles for all gasoline-powered ones in California would reduce smog attributable to highway vehicles by 58 percent and overall by 14-22 percent. California Energy Commission, Air Resources Board, South Coast Air Quality Management District, "Report of the Three-Agency Methanol Task Force," Sacramento, Calif., May 15, 1986.

93. For a discussion, see DeLuchi et al., "Comparative Analysis of Future Transportation Fuels"; California Council for Environmental and Economic Balance, *Alternative Fuels*; "Gasohol Not the Tonic for U.S. Energy Ailments," *Journal of Commerce*, November 9, 1987; California Energy Commission, "Report of the Methanol Task Force." EPA and California state officials disagree about whether pure methanol helps reduce nitrogen oxides; Alson, private communication.

94. Coal contains 1.4 times as much carbon per unit of stored energy as oil; Jim MacKenzie, "Relative Releases of Carbon Dioxide from Several Fuels," World Resources Institute, Washington, D.C., mimeographed, June 10, 1987. For detailed calculations of CO_2 emissions from methanol production, transmission, and use, see Mark DeLuchi et al., "Transportation Fuels and the Greenhouse Effect," University of California, Davis, December 1987. Methanol from coal also produces considerable sulfur dioxide emissions.

95. OECD, *Environmental Effects of Automotive Transport*; DeLuchi et al., "Comparative Analysis of Future Transportation Fuels." On greenhouse gases, see DeLuchi et al., "Transportation Fuels and the Greenhouse Effect"; MacKenzie, "Relative Releases of Carbon Dioxide."

96. DeLuchi et al., "Comparative Analysis of Future Transportation Fuels"; DeLuchi et al., "Transportation Fuels and the Greenhouse Effect."

97. Hoffmann, "Fueling the Future With Hydrogen"; Hoffmann, "Hydrogen: Power to Burn?" Producing hydrogen from coal, however, would produce significant nitrogen and sulfur oxide emissions, and more than double the CO_2 emissions, compared with gasoline vehicles; DeLuchi et al., "Transportation Fuels and the Greenhouse Effect."

98. Gordon MacDonald, Mitre Corporation, personal communication, April 28, 1988.

99. Worldwide fatality figure based on International Road Federation, *World Road Statistics 1981-1985* (Washington, D.C.: 1986) and on MVMA, *Facts and Figures '87*; "The Motorization of the 3rd World," *National Association of Railroad Passengers News*, July 1987.

100. For space needs per car, see James A. Bush, "Would America Have Been Automobilized in a Free Market?" (letter to the editor), *New York Times*, February 10, 1985; U.S. paved area based on Richard Register, "What is an Ecocity?" *Earth Island Journal*, Fall 1987; global average of land devoted to cars from Brown and Jacobson, *The Future of Urbanization*; U.S. urban figure from Kirkpatrick Sale, *Human Scale* (New York: Coward, McCann, & Geoghegan, 1980).

101. Sale, *Human Scale*.

102. Flavin and Durning, *Building on Success*; "Die Blechlawine Soll Unter der Erde Rollen," *Süddeutsche Zeitung*, January 22, 1988; Peter W.G. Newman and Jeffrey R. Kenworthy, "The Use and Abuse of Driving Cycle Research: Clarifying the Relationship Between Traffic Congestion, Energy and Emissions," *Transportation Quarterly*, October 1984; Charles Lockwood and Christopher B. Leinberger, "Los Angeles Comes of Age," *Atlantic Monthly*, January 1988; California Commission quoted in Robert Lindsay, "California Now Sees Cars as a Threat," *New York Times*, April 5, 1988.

103. The Department of Transportation calculated that 1.4 billion gallons were wasted on U.S. highways. An unofficial estimate is that congestion on all other U.S. roads causes a roughly similar amount of fuel to be wasted. Federal Highway Administration, *Quantification of Urban Freeway Congestion and Analysis of Remedial Measures* (Washington, D.C.: Department of Transportation, 1986); Jeffrey Lindley, Department of Transportation, Washington, D.C., private communication, April 19, 1988.

104. "Jam Sessions," *U.S. News and World Report*, September 7, 1987; Christopher B. Leinberger and Charles Lockwood, "How Business is Reshaping America," *Atlantic Monthly*, October 1986.

105. Newman and Kenworthy, "Gasoline Consumption and Cities." The automobile accounts for 80 percent of passenger miles traveled for all purposes in the United States, but only for 57 percent in Japan. In Europe, the share of the automobile in passenger miles traveled is highest in West Germany, where it accounts for about 80 percent. MVMA, *Facts and Figures '87*; Naoki Kuroda, "Japan's Auto Industry," *Journal of Japanese Trade and Industry*, No. 6, 1985; Bundesministerium für Verkehr, *Verkehr in Zahlen 1987*.

106. MVMA, *Facts and Figures '87*.

107. In the United States, some $17 billion in contributions to 1986 highway construction and maintenance funds, or almost one-third, were subsidized; subsidies in the form of municipal services could be as high as $60 billion annually. Furthermore, auto commuters are frequently reimbursed by employers for travel expenses and enjoy free parking at their workplace. "Huge Highway Subsidies . . .," *National Association of Railroad Passengers News*, June 1985; Federal Highway Administration, *Highway Statistics 1986* (Washington, D.C.: U.S. Department of Transportation, 1987); Stanley Hart, "Huge City Subsidies for Autos, Trucks," *California Transit*, July/September 1986. Per-car and per-gallon subsidy estimates are from Stanley Hart, Sierra Club, San Francisco, Calif., private communication, April 12, 1988.

108. Michael Replogle, "Sustainable Transportation Strategies for Third World Development," prepared for session on Human-Powered Transportation and Transportation Planning for Developing Countries, Transport Research Board 1988 Annual Meeting, National Research Council, Washington, D.C.

109. World Bank, *Urban Transport* (Washington, D.C.: 1986).

110. In the United States in 1984, urban rail and bus transit systems used 20 percent less energy per passenger mile than the average car on the road, Amtrak used 40 percent less energy, and intercity buses used less than one-third as much energy. If public transit systems were used to fuller capacity, the advantages would increase further. Holcomb et al., *Transportation Energy Data Book*. On road space requirements, see Frederick C. Dunbar and Richard T. Rapp, "Urban Transport Economics: Analysis for Development Banks," presented at First Annual Meeting, International Mass Transit Association, Washington, D.C., February 16-17, 1986.

111. American Public Transit Association, *1987 Transit Fact Book* (Washington, D.C.: 1987); William S. Kowinski, "There's Still Time to Hop a Trolley—Vintage or Modern," *Smithsonian*, February 1988.

112. The elimination of the interurban rail systems is documented in detail by Bradford Snell, "Report on American Ground Transport," Subcommittee on Antitrust and Monopoly, Senate Judiciary Committee, February 26, 1974; Jonathan Kwitny, "The Great Transportation Conspiracy," *Harpers*, February 1981; Leonard Arrow, "Derailing America—GM's Mark of Excellence," *Environmental Action*, March 16, 1974.

113. American Public Transit Association, *1987 Fact Book*; Kowinski, "There's Still Time to Hop a Trolley."

114. Kathleen Frenchman, "Urban Transport," *South*, November 1987.

115. Citizens for Better Transit, "Multi-Destinational Transit," Portland, Ore., mimeographed, 1977.

116. Michael A. Replogle, *Bicycles and Public Transportation: New Links to Suburban Transit Markets*, 2nd ed. (Washington, D.C.: The Bicycle Federation, 1988).

117. The Chicago Area Transportation Study assessed a number of alternatives to automobile access to public transit. It found that bike-and-ride access would reduce hydrocarbon emissions at a public cost of $311 per ton, compared with $3,937 per ton for a commuter rail-carpool matching service, $96,415 for an express park-and-ride service, and $214,950 for a feeder bus service. Similar differentials were calculated for carbon monoxide reduction costs. See Replogle, *Bicycles and Public Transportation*.

118. Juri Pill, "Land Development: The Latest Panacea for Transit?" *Mass Transit*, January/February 1988.

119. Register, "What is an Ecocity?"; Newman and Kenworthy, "Gasoline Consumption and Cities."

120. Leinberger and Lockwood, "How Business Is Reshaping America"; Philip Langdon, "A Good Place to Live," *Atlantic Monthly*, March 1988.

121. Replogle, "Sustainable Transportation Strategies."

122. Ken Hughes and Michael Replogle, "Sustainable Transportation," *Not Man Apart*, August 1987.

123. Burkhard Horn and Franz-Joseph Götz, "Moving the Third World: Improving Road Transport and Safety in Developing Countries," *OECD Observer*, February/March 1988. Numerous African countries were forced to abandon ambitious plans for road expansion early in their automotive history. A U.N. survey found that between 1974 and 1984, road length decreased in 15 percent of 88 countries surveyed—mostly those in Africa—and remained about the same in another one-quarter. Worldwide, meanwhile, road length increased by 10 percent. United Nations Environment Programme, *Environmental Data Report* (Nairobi: 1987).

124. V. Setty Pendakur, "Formal and Informal Urban Transport in Asia," *CUSO Journal*, December 1987; Brown and Jacobson, *The Future of Urbanization*; Replogle, "Sustainable Transportation Strategies."

125. Replogle, "Sustainable Transportation Strategies."

126. The World Bank accounts for by far the largest share of international development banks' spending on transportation projects. Dunbar and Rapp, "Urban Transport Economics: Analysis for Development Banks"; Replogle, "Sustainable Transportation Strategies"; Hughes and Replogle, "Sustainable Transportation." On the "Africar," see Jonathan Miller, "A Car for All Seasons," *South*, October 1987.

127. Frenchman, "Urban Transport"; Geoffrey Freeman Allen, "Making Tracks on the High Way," *South*, November 1987; Alan Cowell, "People Not Ready to Ride in a Hole in the Ground," *New York Times*, November 12, 1987.

128. Replogle, "Sustainable Transportation Strategies"; Pendakur, "Urban Transport in Asia."

129. Replogle, "Sustainable Transportation Strategies"; Neal R. Peirce, "China's Bike Boom Backward?" *China Daily*, March 9, 1988; "Record Production of 40 Million Bicycles," *China Daily*, January 16, 1988; George Work and Laurence Malone, "Bicycles, Development, and the Third World," *Environment*, January/February 1983.

130. Replogle, "Sustainable Transportation Strategies."

131. André Gorz, *Ecology as Politics* (Boston: South End Press, 1980).

MICHAEL RENNER is a Researcher with Worldwatch Institute. Prior to joining Worldwatch, he was a researcher at the World Policy Institute in New York and a Corliss Lamont Fellow in Economic Conversion at Columbia University. He is a graduate of the University of Amsterdam, where he studied International Relations.

THE WORLDWATCH PAPER SERIES

*Worldwatch Papers 2, 4, 5, 6, 8, 9, 11, 12, 14, 15, 17, 19, 20, 22, 23, 24, 26, 27, 32, and 37 are out of print.

Bulk Copies (any combination of titles)   **Single Copy** $4.00
        2-5: $3.00 each   6-20: $2.00 each   21 or more: $1.00 each

Calendar Year Subscription (1988 subscription begins with Paper 81)   U.S. $25.00 ___

Make check payable to Worldwatch Institute
1776 Massachusetts Avenue NW, Washington, D.C. 20036 USA

Enclosed is my check for U.S. $ ___

_____
name
_____
address
_____
city   **state**   **zip/country**